KINDERGARTEN

LOOK & LEARN

Kolbe
ACADEMY PRESS®

Napa, California

© Kolbe Academy Press 2024
All Rights Reserved

Printed for:

K | KOLBE
A | ACADEMY

1600 F Street
Napa, CA 94559-1034

Tel: (707) 255-6499
Fax: (707) 256-4313

To purchase this product visit **books.kolbe.org**

$\mathcal{K}$indergarten is a time to enjoy the wonder and beauty of Creation with which God has surrounded us. It is a time to teach children to connect with the past and immerse themselves in their life within the Church.

The Look & Learn text gives students a first exposure to the beauty that surrounds them. This book provides key information needed to complete the journals. In our Kindergarten Journal and Art Journal, the student is given simple worksheets to concretize some of the simple, basic facts they are learning. In the Art Journal, they practice the first principles that make art beautiful.

Through memorizing and practicing the words of the Baltimore Catechism and the words of Scripture, students will be drawn into the cultural heritage and the importance of order and precision. In art, the same is true. The students will be drawn into the beauty of the art, and will practice and see the order and the principles that make it so. In the poetry sections, students are led to see the beauty of words.

In science, students are focused on learning about God's creation. To look at formal and final causes and to wonder and rest in that wonder is our goal. Our approach to history is also very intentional. Students follow the liturgical year as it is their year and by what they measure time. In Preschool the intention was to introduce the students to the world they live in; here they are introduced to the world of their first friend: Jesus. The students are drawn to make a connection between the world that Jesus lived in and their own world.

lesson 1

Assumption of Mary

Art by Palma il Vecchio (c. 1513)

- What colors do you see in this painting?

- Who are the other figures in the painting? What are they doing?

- Look at the sky around Mary. It is gold instead of blue! What do you think that represents?

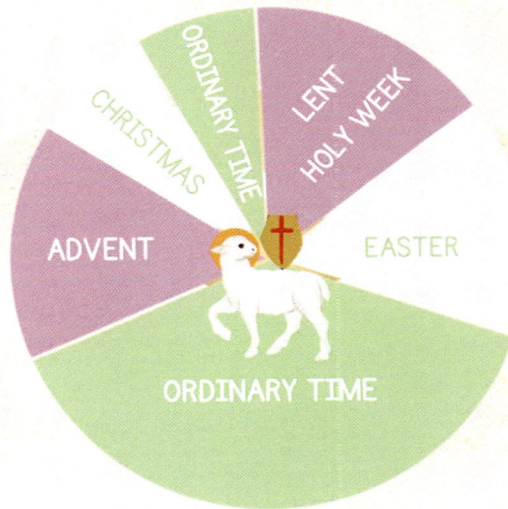

Ordinary Time

Just as there are seasons in nature, there are seasons in the Church when we celebrate special events like Advent, Christmas, Lent, Easter, and Ordinary Time. These are called liturgical seasons. When we celebrate the liturgical seasons, we celebrate the birth, life, death, and resurrection of Jesus.

The Church represents each liturgical season with a special color. Green is a symbol for growing, purple is a symbol for preparation, and white & gold are a symbol for celebration.

Ordinary Time is a season we celebrate twice each year – after the Christmas season until Lent and after the Easter season until Advent. Ordinary Time is a time for growing. Just as plants grow in nature, this is a time for us to grow in holiness.

The liturgical color of Ordinary Time is green. If you see the priest at Mass wearing green vestments, then you know it must be Ordinary Time!

Can you find Ordinary Time on the liturgical calendar? What is your favorite liturgical season? Why?

Needed to Grow:

1  SOIL

2

3

cactus

mushroom

Common Plants in My Yard

All plants need **soil, sun, and water** to grow. But not all plants are the same. Some plants, like the cactus, need lots of sun and only a little water to survive. Other plants, like the mushroom, need lots of water and only a little sun.

Different plants grow in different parts of the world because the amount of soil, sun, and water a plant will get depends on the <u>climate</u>. Climate is the typical weather a certain place experiences. Plants that need lots of sun and little water will grow in dry climates, while plants that need more water and less sun will grow in rainy climates.

> What plants grow where you live? Go to your backyard or a nearby park and make a list of the plants you discover. Why do you think those plants grow near you?

lesson 1

> **I**n the beginning was the Word, and the Word was with God, and the Word was God.
> -John 1:1

In the Beginning...

- Usually, we think of a word as something we see written on paper or hear with our ears. But here the Word is a person. Who could that be? It is Jesus, the second Person of the Holy Trinity.

- Jesus existed before the earth, the sun, and the stars were created. In fact, He created the sun, moon, and stars because He is God!

Childhood of Christ

Art by Gerrit van Honthorst (c. 1620)

- What do you notice first in this painting?

- Whose faces can you see better: the people in the foreground or the people in the background? Why is that?

- Tell me a story about what you see in this painting.

HISTORY

Jesus' Life as a Little Child

Ordinary Time

We remember that beautiful Scripture verse from our first religion lesson. It told us that Jesus is God and existed before all of Creation.

Because He loves us, Jesus became man. He did this to make us children of God and help us be with Him forever in heaven. But Jesus did not start out as a man. Just like you, He was born a baby.

When Jesus was a little boy, He lived with Mary and Joseph in Nazareth. He did not have any brothers or sisters, but their home was filled with love. Joseph worked as a carpenter, a person who builds things with wood.

Mary and Joseph taught Jesus how to read, do chores, and pray their family prayers. As a child, Jesus was always obedient, and He grew in strength and wisdom.

How is your life similar to Jesus' childhood? How is it different?

lesson 2

cypress tree

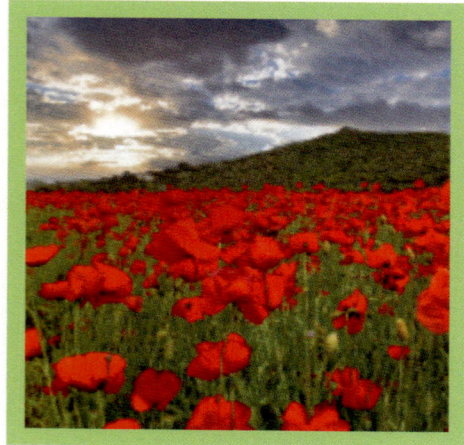

poppies

Common Plants in Jesus' Land

We call the place where Jesus lived the Holy Land. It is located in the country of Israel. The Holy Land has <u>hot and dry summers</u> and <u>cold and wet winters</u>. Because of this, some plants in the Holy Land grow in the summer and others grow in the winter.

The cypress tree and olive tree are common in Jesus' land. They do not need much water to grow, so they can survive the hot and dry summers.

Flowers like lilies, daisies, and poppies also grow in the Holy Land. They need more water to survive and cannot grow when it is very hot, so they grow in the winter and spring when it is cold and rainy.

In Jesus' land different plants grow in different seasons. Does that happen where you live? What plants do you see in the summer and what plants do you see in the winter? What is different about the soil, sun, and water in those seasons?

Baltimore Catechism

Question 1: Who made the world?

Answer: God made the world.

Question 2: Who is God?

Answer: God is the Creator of heaven and earth and all things.

Still Life of Grapes, Lemons, Cherries, Oysters, and a Bread Roll

Art by Alexander Coosemans (1627-1689)

- What foods do you see in this painting?

- Can you tell from this painting how each food might feel if you touched it? Which foods would be smooth? Which foods would be rough? What makes you think that?

- If you were to draw a still life painting, what foods would you draw?

bread and wine

fish

lamb

Food and Drink in Jesus' Time

Ordinary Time

When Jesus lived His earthly life, big supermarkets like we have today did not exist. The food people ate came from the plants and animals that lived nearby. The Bible tells us about some of the food and drink in Jesus' time.

Grains like wheat and barley grew in Jesus' land and were used to make bread. The Bible tells us that Jesus ate bread. Grapevines were also common in Jesus' land. They used those grapes to make wine, and the Bible tells us that Jesus drank wine.

Jesus lived near a body of water called the Sea of Galilee. Some of His friends were fishermen and caught fish to eat. The Bible tells us that Jesus cooked and ate the fish that His friends caught in their boats.

The Bible also tells us that Jesus ate lamb. Shepherds in Jesus' land cared for sheep and used the sheep's wool for clothing and its meat for food.

Some foods (like peanut butter) and some drinks (like coffee) weren't invented in Jesus' time. We know Jesus did not eat peanut butter or drink coffee because they did not exist yet.

> Do you remember some of the foods that Jesus ate?
> What are some of the foods He did not eat?

farm corn

fruit tree

backyard garden

Food From Plants in My Local Land

Much of the food we eat comes from plants. Sometimes those plants are grown on a farm. A farmer grows lots of the same plant—like corn, wheat, rice, or lettuce—and sells it to people who use it to make food.

Sometimes food grows on trees. Fruits like apples, lemons, oranges, avocados, and bananas grow on trees. Sometimes those trees can be found in an orchard, and sometimes they can be found in your own yard or local park.

Sometimes food is grown in a backyard garden or community garden. Plants are grown and taken care of until the plant or its fruit is ready to eat. Vegetables like tomatoes, zucchini, spinach, and pumpkins are often grown in a garden.

Sometimes food can be found from plants in the wild. Some vegetables like asparagus grow near fields, and some fruits like berries grow in the forest. You should never eat food in the wild unless a grown-up tells you it is safe to eat. Some wild plants can make you very sick.

What food comes from the plants where you live?
Where do you get the food that grows near you?

lesson 3

Baltimore Catechism

Art by Michelangelo (c. 1511)

Question 3: What is man?

Answer: Man is a creature composed of body and soul and made to the image and likeness of God.

The Sermon on the Mount

Art by Fra Angelico (1437)

- What colors do you see in this painting?

- What is Jesus doing in this painting?

- The people in this painting have gold circles around their heads. Can you guess what they are and what they mean?

- The shadows and lines in the sky and rocks create arcs and a circle around Jesus and the crowd. The painter even painted the crowd in a close circle around Jesus. This helps draw your eye to Jesus as the most important part of the painting. Can you use your finger to trace some of the lines that make circles and arcs and help us focus on Jesus?

lesson 4

Parables: Stories Jesus Told

Art by Carl Christian Vogel von Vogelstein (c. 1868)

Sometimes it can be hard to really understand something, but when we hear about it in a story then suddenly it is easy to understand. A story that teaches us something is called a "parable". The Bible shows us that Jesus told lots of parables.

Do you find it difficult to imagine what God is like? Jesus knew that His friends had a hard time understanding God, so Jesus told parables, or teaching stories, about Him. In these stories Jesus said that God is like a good shepherd who knows the name of every single sheep because He loves them so much. He is like a shepherd who never abandons His sheep. And if one gets lost, He will go searching for that sheep to bring it home! These stories help us understand that God knows us and loves us very much.

Jesus also told his friends about the Kingdom of Heaven, because Jesus wants us to be with Him forever in heaven. His friends had a hard time understanding what that meant, so Jesus told them parables about the Kingdom of Heaven. He told stories about how plants grow and how bread is made to help them understand that the Kingdom of Heaven is real even though we can't see it. He told them a story about a pearl that was worth more than any other treasure. This story helps us understand how precious and important the Kingdom of Heaven is.

In the coming weeks, we'll read some of the parables that Jesus told.

Can you think of a story that has taught you something?

wheat

olive tree

fig tree

Food From Plants in Jesus' Land

Wheat is a plant that grew in the land where Jesus lived. During Jesus' earthly life, they did not have tractors like we do today, so farmers would prepare the soil and then scatter the seeds in the field. The seeds that fell in the soil prepared by the farmers would grow into wheat plants. People used the wheat to make bread. This was a common food in Jesus' land.

Olive trees are another common plant in the Holy Land. Olives grow on trees and in Jesus' time they were used mainly for their oil. The oil was used for food, to light lamps, and to give blessings during holy ceremonies.

There are many large trees in Jesus' land that also produce food. One example is the fig tree. It produces a fruit called the fig, which has a sweet taste and a squishy texture. Another large tree that grew in Jesus' land is the mustard tree. It produces mustard seeds that are used as a spice in different dishes.

Do any of these plants grow where you live?

What food grows in the ground or on the trees where you live?

Baltimore Catechism

Question 4: Why did God make you?

Answer: God made me to know Him, to love Him, and to serve Him in this world, and to be happy with Him for ever in heaven.

lesson 5

Illuminated Manuscript from the Commentary on the Epistles of St. Paul

French work by Gilbert de la Porrée (c. 1145)

- Find the fancy letter on this page and trace the letter with your finger.

- What details do you notice on the letter?

- This letter P is for the first letter in the name Paul. What is the first letter of your name?

lesson 5

The Parable of the Good Shepherd

Art by Bernhard Plockhorst (c. 1825)

"He Knows His Sheep By Name"

When Jesus lived on this earth, He traveled throughout the Holy Land with His friends. People were drawn to Him, and everyone wanted to listen and know more about Him. One day He shared a parable to help them understand Him. Jesus told His friends:

"He who enters by the door is the shepherd of the sheep. To him the gatekeeper opens; the sheep hear his voice, and he calls his own sheep by name and leads them out. When he has brought out all his own, he goes before them, and the sheep follow him, for they know his voice. A stranger they will not follow, but they will flee from him, for they do not know the voice of strangers.

I am the good shepherd. The good shepherd lays down his life for the sheep. . . I am the good shepherd; I know my own and my own know me, as the Father knows me and I know the Father; and I lay down my life for the sheep." (John 10:1-5, 11-15)

> **In this parable what did you hear?**
> **What do the sheep do?**
> **How do they know to follow the shepherd?**

Read the Scripture passage again. After the second reading ask:

> **What does the shepherd do for his sheep?**
> **How well does he know them?**
> **I wonder who these special sheep could be?**

lesson 5

Let's Learn About Sheep

Jesus used the image of sheep and shepherds in His parable of the good shepherd because sheep were important animals in His time. They are important animals in our time too!

Sheep grow soft wool on their bodies to keep them warm, and we use that wool to make coats, scarves, and sweaters to keep us warm. Sheep are usually shorn in the spring when the weather is warm so they have time to grow back their wool covering (which is called a fleece) before the cold weather returns.

Sheep are also a good source of food. We use their milk to make cheese and enjoy lamb meat from sheep raised for food.

Sheep are raised in a group together. A group of sheep is called a flock. They mainly eat grass, and you will usually see them grazing in a field. In the winter when there is less grass in the field, they are often fed hay or grains.

> Why is the sheep considered a useful animal?

lesson 5

He calls his own sheep by name and leads them out.
-John 10:3

lesson 6

ICH BIN GUTE   DER HIRT

Mosaic of Christ as the Good Shepherd

Central Cemetery of Kufstein, Austria (19th century)

- What do you notice first in this artwork?

- Where are the sheep on the ground guiding you to look?

- Sometimes artists use "clues" to help the viewer recognize the religious story or depiction. What "clues"' tell you this is an image of Jesus and not just a regular shepherd? (Hint: Why is Jesus wearing a royal robe and a halo as a shepherd? What does it say about who He is?)

- A mosaic is made by taking small pieces of material and putting them together to make an image. Look closely and see if you can spot the small pieces that form this picture. (Hint: they look like teeny-tiny squares.)

lesson 6

The Parable of the Lost Sheep

Art by James Tissot (late 19ᵗʰ century)

Have you ever lost something special to you? How did you feel when that happened? What did you do? You probably searched for it and were so excited when you found it!

Jesus told a parable to help us understand how God responds when we stray far from Him. His parable helps us understand that each and every one of us is special to God. He seeks us when we are lost and is so excited when we are reunited with Him! Let's read this parable of the lost sheep:

> "What man among you having a hundred sheep and losing one of them would not leave the ninety-nine in the desert and go after the lost one until he finds it?
>
> And when he does find it, he sets it on his shoulders with great joy and, upon his arrival home, he calls together his friends and neighbors and says to them, 'Rejoice with me because I have found my lost sheep.'
>
> I tell you, in just the same way there will be more joy in heaven over one sinner who repents than over ninety-nine righteous people who have no need of repentance." (Luke 15:4-7)

What did you hear in this parable?

How do you think the shepherd felt?

How do you think the sheep felt?

I wonder who had more joy, the shepherd or the sheep who was found?

Shepherds in the Holy Land

Art by John Rogers Herbert (1877)

As we learned in the last science lesson, sheep were important animals in Jesus' land. Flocks of sheep lived all over the Holy Land, grazing in the pasture or drinking from streams.

Because sheep were so useful, shepherds in the Holy Land had a very important job. But it was a difficult one.

It was the shepherd's job to lead the sheep to pastures to eat and streams to drink. There were usually many sheep in a flock, and sometimes the sheep didn't want to follow the shepherd—they wanted to go their own way! It was the shepherd's job to make sure all the sheep stayed together and got the food and water they needed to be healthy.

It was also the shepherd's job to protect the sheep from <u>predators</u>. Predators are animals that hunt other animals for food. Wolves, bears, and lions eat sheep. The shepherd protected the sheep from these predators and sometimes had to fight them off. King David was a shepherd when he was young, and he killed a lion and a bear that were trying to eat his father's sheep!

Would you have liked to be a shepherd in Jesus' land?

lesson 6

Baltimore Catechism

Question 5: What must we do to save our souls?

Answer: To save our souls, we must worship God by faith, hope, and charity; that is, we must believe in Him, hope in Him, and love Him with all our heart.

Landscape with Large Tree

Art by Reuben Oliver Luckenbach (c. 1860)

- What do you notice first in this painting?

- Can you find the fence in this painting? Is it in the foreground, midground, or background?

- Can you show me what is in sunlight and what is in shadow?

- What would it feel like to sit under this tree? What sounds might you hear?

lesson 7

The Parable of the Mustard Seed

Did you notice what color the priest's vestments were at Mass on Sunday? They were probably green because we are in Ordinary Time! This is a season when adults and children grow in faith and love for God. In the Kingdom of God, size doesn't matter. God has the power to make something very tiny grow into something great.

We remember that Jesus often spoke in parables to share the Kingdom of God with His people. One day when Jesus was teaching, He said to His friends:

"The kingdom of heaven is like a mustard seed that a person took and sowed in a field. It is the smallest of all the seeds, yet when full grown it is the largest of plants. It becomes a large bush, and the birds of the sky come and dwell in its branches." (Matthew 13:31-32)

What did you hear?

What does Jesus say the Kingdom of God is like?

What is this seed like?

What happens to it? Whose power could make this happen?

What does Jesus want us to know about the Kingdom of God?

Plants Grow From Seeds

Seeds are amazing little bundles of life. They may be small, but everything a plant needs to start growing is packed inside.

The outside of the seed is called the seed coat. It is hard and protects the seed until it starts growing. The inside of the seed contains food, which provides all the energy and growing materials needed until the plant can push its way above the soil.

Seeds come in many different shapes and sizes. Usually the larger a seed is, the bigger the plant will grow. But that is not always the case. Mustard seeds are so small they can fit on the tip of your finger. Peach seeds are much bigger than mustard seeds, but both peach trees and mustard trees grow to be about the same size.

Seeds are found in the fruit of flowering plants. If you eat fruits like apples, oranges, or watermelon, you may find a seed inside while you're eating.

Each seed has the potential to grow into a new plant. If you carve pumpkins in the fall, think about how many pumpkin seeds are inside. There may be hundreds. Each one of those seeds has the potential to grow into a new pumpkin plant.

Find three pieces of fruit in your house that have seeds inside.

Where are the seeds in each fruit?

How are they different?

How are they similar?

INDVIMINI : VIRTVTE,EXALTO

Baltimore Catechism

Question 6: How shall we know the things which we are to believe?

Answer: We shall know the things which we are to believe from the Catholic Church, through which God speaks to us.

The Archangel Raphael and Tobias

Art by Tiziano Vecellio (early 16th century)

- What do you see in the foreground? What do you see in the background?

- Notice that the background is blurry and the foreground is clear. This is a clue the artist gives that the foreground is close and the background is far away.

- Where do you think the travelers are going? Tell me a story about what you see in this painting.

- Can you find two animals in this painting? Point to them.

lesson 8

The Parable of the Growing Seed

Do you remember what liturgical season we are in? We are in Ordinary Time, which is a time for growing! We listened to a parable about growing and the Kingdom of God. What did Jesus say the Kingdom of God is like? Jesus told another parable about the kingdom to His friends. Let's listen:

"This is how it is with the kingdom of God; it is as if a man were to scatter seed on the land and would sleep and rise night and day and the seed would sprout and grow, he knows not how.

Of its own accord the land yields fruit, first the blade, then the ear, then the full grain in the ear. And when the grain is ripe, he wields the sickle at once, for the harvest has come." (Mark 4:26-29)

What stood out to you in this parable?

What does Jesus want us to know about the Kingdom of God?

Could this be the same power at work that makes the mustard seed grow?

How Plants Grow

In the parable of the growing seed, Jesus says a seed will sprout and grow, even if we don't know how it happens. But we can learn how seeds grow into plants! Today we will learn the <u>life cycle of a plant.</u>

Do you remember in the last science lesson when we learned a seed is packed with everything it needs to start growing? The seed consists of food, which gives it energy to grow, and an <u>embryo</u>, which is a tiny plant with a stem, leaves, and parts to make roots.

If a seed gets good soil, water, and sun then it will begin to grow! The embryo will break out of its protective covering—the stem will push up toward the light and the roots will push down in the soil. Sunlight and soil give the plant the <u>nutrients</u> it needs to keep growing!

The job of the roots is to take in water and nutrients from the soil, and the job of the leaves is to take in sunlight, which the plant can turn into food. As it gets bigger, the plant will grow more leaves and the roots will spread deeper into the soil. This will help the plant get more sun, water, and nutrients. Many plants grow flowers, which are important for producing new seeds. The seeds that come from the plant's flower or fruit can then grow into new plants, and the cycle continues again.

What are two ways a plant can get the nutrients it needs to grow?

Coment li apostre font la credo.

Baltimore Catechism

Question 7: Where shall we find the chief truths which the Church teaches?

Answer: We shall find the chief truths which the Church teaches in the Apostles' Creed.

lesson 9

Still Life of Breads

Art by Ilya Mashkov (1912)

- What do you first notice about this painting?

- Many kinds of bread are shown in this painting. Which one would you like to eat?

- What do you notice in the background?

- In this painting the artist is more concerned with light and color than the details of the object he is painting. See how the pieces of bread don't have much detail so you can't tell if they are soft, hard, or crumbly? But notice where there is light and shadow. Point to some places where you see shadow on the bread. Point to some places you see light.

The Parable of the Leaven

In Jesus' time, bread was the main food eaten at every meal. But most people did not get their bread from a grocery store. They made it in their homes. The ingredients they used to make bread were flour and water. Sometimes they would add yeast to make leavened bread, and sometimes they did not add yeast and made unleavened bread.

Unleavened bread, which is bread without yeast, is flat, and the dough is firm. But when yeast is added to the flour and water, the dough rises and is soft like a pillow. Leavened bread is rounder in shape and soft inside. The people of Jesus' time knew well the way yeast transforms dough from flat and firm to soft and puffy.

Jesus used the image of yeast transforming bread to help His friends understand the Kingdom of God. He spoke to them another parable:

"The kingdom of heaven is like yeast that a woman took and mixed with three measures of wheat flour until the whole batch was leavened." (Matthew 13:33)

What stood out to you in this parable?

What does this parable tell you about the Kingdom of God?

How Dough Grows

The parable of the leaven uses the image of yeast transforming dough. Today we will learn how yeast reacts with dough to make soft and tasty bread!

Yeast is a kind of leaven. The word leavening comes from the Latin word levare, which means "to lift up, to make rise." Bread recipes always have leavening to make the dough rise.

Yeast is a living organism that can be found all around us. The yeast we typically use for bread may look like little seeds, but they are actually alive!

A simple bread recipe starts with flour, warm water, yeast, salt, and sugar. Do you like to eat sugar? Yeast does too! When it is in a warm, moist environment and given some sugar, yeast will gobble it right up. When yeast eats sugar, it produces carbon dioxide.

Have you seen the little bubbles in soda pop or sparkling water? Those are made from carbon dioxide. When yeast eats sugar and produces carbon dioxide, it creates little air bubbles in the bread like the bubbles you see in soda pop. The air bubbles get trapped in the flour mixture. As the air bubbles try to escape, they cause the dough to rise and get bigger.

If you break open a loaf of bread you can see small holes in the bread. That shows you where the air bubbles were!

What is one thing you learned about yeast today?

lesson 9

The kingdom of heaven is like yeast that a woman took and mixed with three measures of wheat flour until the whole batch was leavened.

–Matthew 13:33

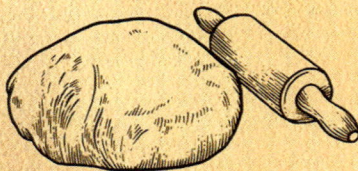

lesson 10

Luke the Evangelist

Illuminated Gospel Book, unknown artist (c. 860)

- What colors do you see in this painting?

- Can you find an ox with wings? Point to it.

- The Gospels tell us about Jesus' life on earth. St. Luke wrote one of the Gospels. This painting is from an old book that has the Gospels of Matthew, Mark, Luke, and John. What would you draw to make a book of the Gospels beautiful?

- St. Luke is holding a book and sitting next to a basket of scrolls. Do you know why?

The Parable of the Pearl

What is the most expensive thing you can think of? In Jesus' time, a pearl was one of the most expensive things anyone could own. Today, we know how to grow pearls, and we have SCUBA equipment to dive for pearls. But in Jesus' time, pearls were extremely rare. If someone owned a pearl, it was a sign they were rich and important.

The Kingdom of God is very important. We know this because Jesus talked about it a lot. Let's listen to something else Jesus shared with His friends about the Kingdom of God:

> *"The kingdom of heaven is like a merchant searching for fine pearls. When he finds a pearl of great price, he goes and sells all that he has and buys it."* (Matthew 13:45-46)

What stood out to you in this parable?

How Pearls are Made

While most gems are found in the earth, pearls are made from living creatures! A mollusk is a type of animal with a soft body and a hard shell that protects its body. Clams, mussels, and oysters are all examples of mollusks. Any mollusk with a shell can produce a pearl, and pearls can be produced in both fresh water and salt water.

When you cut your skin on something, your body produces a scab. This hard crust over the cut protects your body from germs while your skin heals. In a similar way, when a mollusk gets a grain of sand, a small fish, or a piece of food trapped inside it, the mollusk protects itself by wrapping the object in a smooth substance called nacre. Nacre is a strong substance that reflects light and color in a shimmering way. It is what pearls are made of. As many layers of nacre are produced to surround the unwelcome object, a pearl forms.

While pearls are usually white and round, they can come in all different shapes and sizes. We do not yet know what causes pearls to be certain colors, but there are black, gray, red, blue, and green pearls. Pearls that are round are the most valuable, but they can also come in uneven shapes.

What is one thing you learned about pearls today?

lesson 10

Baltimore Catechism

The Holy Trinity by Pietro Novelli (17th century)

Question: What is God?

Answer: God is a spirit infinitely perfect.

Ordinary Time

lesson 11

The Hidden Treasure

Art by Sir John Everett Millais (c. 1860)

- What colors do you see in this painting?

- What do you see in the foreground? In the midground? In the background?

- What is the man looking down at?

- How do you think the man feels about what he has found? How would you feel if you found treasure hidden in the ground?

lesson 11

The Parable of the Hidden Treasure

In Jesus' time the type of land a person owned made a big difference in how much money they could make. Many of the people in Jesus' time had a job that involved producing food. There were farmers who grew plants for food and farmers who raised animals for food. If a person had land that was good for growing, they could grow more plants and feed their animals lots of good grass. If they had land that was not good for growing, they would have a hard time producing food or making money. Valuable land was very important.

We know that the Kingdom of God was very important to Jesus. He told parables to help people understand more about it. What have we already heard? We read the parable about a merchant finding a pearl of great price. Jesus told His friends another parable:

The kingdom of heaven is like a treasure buried in a field, which a person finds and hides again, and out of joy goes and sells all that he has and buys that field." (Matthew 13:44)

What did the person do when he found the treasure?

How did he feel?

lesson 11

Rocks and Minerals

Fresh Water

Salt Water

Fresh Water vs. Salt Water

In the last science lesson we learned about pearls and read that they can grow in both fresh water and salt water. Salt water is water with lots of rock salt in it. Most of the water on earth is salt water found in the oceans.

Fresh water is found in rivers and streams and lakes. This water comes from rain, snow, and underground springs. It does not have very much salt in it. The water in rivers and streams doesn't stay in one place. It moves and travels and eventually empties into an ocean. On its journey to the ocean, fresh water picks up rocks and minerals and carries them along. All the rivers in all the world emptying rocks and minerals into the ocean makes the ocean very salty. That is why we call ocean water salt water.

What is different between salt water and fresh water?
Where is fresh water found? Where is salt water found?
Why is the ocean so salty?

lesson 11

Scripture Review

"The kingdom of heaven is like yeast that a woman took and mixed with three measures of wheat flour until the whole batch was leavened."
(Matthew 13:33)

"In the beginning was the Word, and the Word was with God, and the Word was God." *(John 1:1)*

"He calls his own sheep by name and leads them out." *(John 10:3)*

lesson 12

Communion of Saints

Landauer Altar
Art by Albrecht Dürer (1511)

- What do you notice first in this painting?

- Can you point to the angels?

- Notice how some people look close up and some people look far away. But they are all on a flat painting! This is called <u>linear perspective</u>. The artist draws figures larger to appear close and smaller to make them look far away. Can you point to a figure that looks close? Can you point to a figure that looks far away?

lesson 12

Map View

Surface View

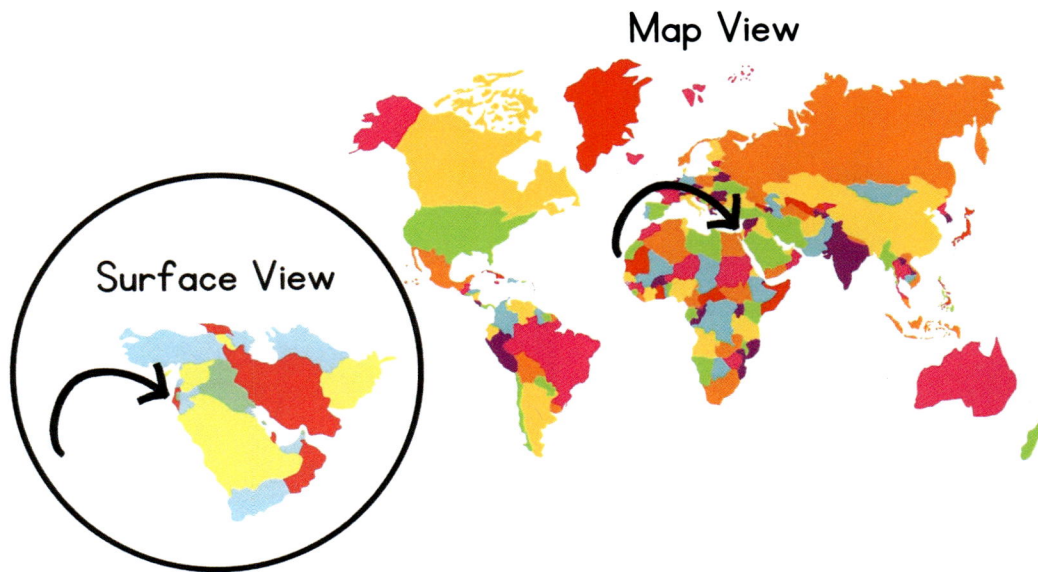

Where Jesus Lived

Jesus lived in a place called Israel. It is a part of a faraway land called Asia. It is located along a beautiful sea called the Mediterranean Sea. Even though it is tiny, it has many different types of landscapes. In Israel, you can find the seacoast, snowy mountains, deserts, forests, and fields.

Many places in Israel may be familiar to you from the Bible. Cities like Nazareth, where Jesus was raised, and Jerusalem, where Jesus died and rose from the dead, are located in Israel. The Red Sea, where Moses and the Israelites crossed, and the Jordan River, where Jesus was baptized, can also be found in Israel. Many people from all over the world travel to Israel each year to walk in the land where Jesus lived!

See where the arrow is pointing on the map above.

Can you find Israel on a globe?

Can you find where you live on the map above?

Lion

Gazelle

Common Animals in Jesus' Land

The Bible mentions many different animals that lived in Jesus' land. We have already learned about some of those animals, like sheep and fish. Sheep and fish are still common animals in Israel and an important source of food.

Today, some wild animals found in Jesus' land are types of deer called the gazelle and the Persian fallow deer. There are many types of bats, lizards, and predators like the striped hyena and the Arabian wolf. Many animals in Jesus' land are endangered. When an animal is endangered, that means there are not many members left, and they are in danger of dying out.

Some animals mentioned in the Bible once lived in Jesus' land but no longer live there. In Jesus' time, there were lions, alligators, cheetahs, and brown bears in Israel. But those animals are not found in Israel today. That means they are extinct there. When an animal is extinct, it means there are no more living members of that animal.

Can you name an animal found in Jesus' land today?

Can you name an animal that used to live in Jesus' land but doesn't anymore?

What does it mean if an animal is endangered?

lesson 12

Baltimore Catechism

St. Robert Bellarmine writing the first catechism

1. **Who made the world?** *(God made the world.)*

2. **Who is God?** *(God is the Creator of heaven and earth and all things.)*

3. **What is man?** *(Man is a creature composed of body and soul and made to the image and likeness of God.)*

4. **Why did God make you?** *(God made me to know Him, to love Him, and to serve Him in this world, and to be happy with Him for ever in heaven.)*

5. **What must we do to save our souls?** *(To save our souls, we must worship God by faith, hope, and charity; that is, we must believe in Him, hope in Him, and love Him with all our heart.)*

6. **How shall we know the things which we are to believe?** *(We shall know the things which we are to believe from the Catholic Church, through which God speaks to us.)*

7. **Where shall we find the chief truths which the Church teaches?** *(We shall find the chief truths which the Church teaches in the Apostles' Creed.)*

8. **What is God?** *(God is a spirit infinitely perfect.)*

lesson 13

Christ Crowned with Thorns

Art by Hans Holbein the Elder (1501)

- What colors stand out to you in this painting?

- What do you think is happening here?

- How do you think the people in the crowd are feeling? How do you think Jesus is feeling? Why do you think that?

- Notice the gold around Jesus' head. What do you think that represents?

lesson 13

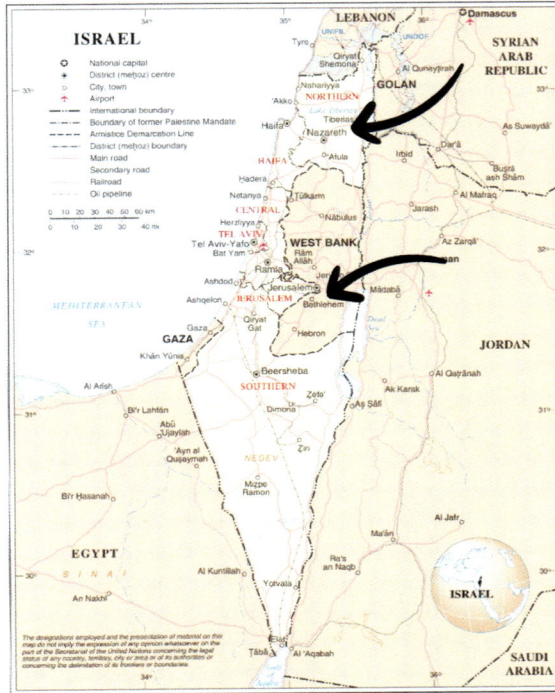

How Maps Help Us

Maps help us understand where certain places are. Maps of countries and cities help us see where we are and where we want to go. They can help us see how far apart two places are from each other and what roads to take to get there.

The map above shows the land where Jesus lived. The Bible tells us that before Jesus was born, Mary and Joseph traveled from their home in Nazareth to Bethlehem.

Point to the top arrow on the map. It points to Nazareth, where Jesus grew up. Now find the bottom arrow on the map. It points to Bethlehem, where Jesus was born. See how far apart they are from each other. The map shows us that Mary and Joseph had to travel more than one hundred miles to get to Bethlehem!

How do maps help us?

Think of a city you would like to visit. Now look at a map to see how far away it is from your home.

lesson 13

Common Animals in My Land

We learned what animals lived in Jesus' land both today and during His time on earth. Now think about what animals live in your land. To help, let's look at some different types of animals in the world.

Insects: There are so many insects in the world! Insects have three parts on their bodies, six legs, and two antennae. Sometimes they have wings. Ants, bees, butterflies, and grasshoppers are all insects. What insects live near you?

Birds: Birds are animals with feathers, wings, and beaks. They lay eggs. Birds can be large or small. Hawks are very big, and hummingbirds are very small. What birds live near you?

Mammals: Mammals are animals that have hair or fur, drink their mothers' milk as babies, and are born alive (not from eggs). Squirrels, foxes, deer, mice, rabbits, and bears are examples of mammals. What mammals live near you?

Reptiles: Reptiles are animals with scales on their bodies instead of fur or feathers. Some lay eggs, but others give birth to live young. Snakes, lizards, and crocodiles are examples of reptiles. What reptiles live near you?

lesson 13

Fatherhood
Art by Viktor Mikhaylovich Vasnetsov (1907)

Baltimore Catechism

Question 9: Had God a beginning?

Answer: God had no beginning; He always was and He always will be.

The First Thanksgiving at Plymouth

Art by Jennie Augusta Brownscombe (1914)

- What is happening in this painting?
- Tell me what you see in the foreground. What do you see in the midground?
- What do you see in the background?
- What do you think the man standing up at the table is doing?
- Can you find water in this painting?

lesson 14

The First Thanksgiving

More than four hundred years ago, a group of people traveled by ship from a country called England. They were looking for a place to live where they could worship God the way they wanted. The ship was called the Mayflower and the people were called pilgrims. They heard about a "New World" across the ocean, and they wanted to live there. They landed at Plymouth Rock in 1620.

But the "New World" was not new. People had lived there for thousands of years. These Native Americans knew the land well and had fished, hunted, and planted food there for many years. The pilgrims were new to the land and were not able to find good food and shelter at first. Many pilgrims did not survive the first winter in the New World.

After their first winter in Plymouth, the pilgrims became friends with a Native American tribe called the Wampanoag. The Wampanoag knew all about the land and taught the pilgrims how to grow crops. That year, the pilgrims grew and hunted enough food to last them through the winter. They celebrated by sharing a feast with the Wampanoag that lasted three days. They thanked God for the many blessings He had given them. This was the very first Thanksgiving.

What did you hear?

What would you thank God for if you were at the first Thanksgiving?

About Turkeys

We don't know if the pilgrims and Native Americans ate turkey at the first Thanksgiving, but most people eat turkey at Thanksgiving today. Turkeys are birds, which means they have wings, feathers, and beaks. They lay eggs. Turkeys are large birds, and they have large feathers on their backside they puff up to get the attention of other turkeys.

Turkeys live in forests and can be found in most of North America, and parts of Mexico. They search for food in open spaces of the forest, where they can eat leaves, grasses, fruits, berries, and insects.

Turkeys make a sound called a gobble. They make these sounds to communicate with other turkeys. Another way turkeys communicate is through their snood. A snood is a long piece of flesh that grows from a turkey's forehead, and it turns red if the turkey is angry. If you see a turkey with some red over its beak, be sure to leave it alone!

What is one thing you learned about turkeys today?

Baltimore Catechism

Question 10: Is there but one God?

Answer: Yes; there is but one God.

Preparing for Christmas

Art by Francis William Edmonds (1851)

- What are the men in this painting doing? How are they preparing for Christmas?

- Do you think the scene in this painting is warm or cold? Point out the signs that show you.

- These men are preparing for Christmas by plucking turkeys. How does your family prepare for Christmas?

Advent

Introduction to Advent

Do you remember when we learned about the different liturgical seasons—Advent, Christmas, Lent, Easter, and Ordinary Time? We have been in Ordinary Time so far this school year, and the next liturgical season is Advent!

At Mass you will notice it is Advent because the priest wears purple. Purple is a sign of preparation, and Advent is a time of preparation for the birth of Jesus. We don't just prepare for Christmas with decorations and presents. We prepare our hearts for the coming of Jesus!

Advent is a time when we look forward to the celebration of Jesus' first coming as a baby many, many years ago. In the readings at Mass, we hear how God told His people that a great light would come into the darkness of the world. Who could this great light be?

Jesus told us He will come again and welcome all His friends into His kingdom. We want to be ready to welcome Jesus into our hearts and to find God's light in the world. Advent is the time to get ready!

What is one thing you learned about Advent today?

What is one way you can prepare your heart to welcome Jesus?

lesson 15

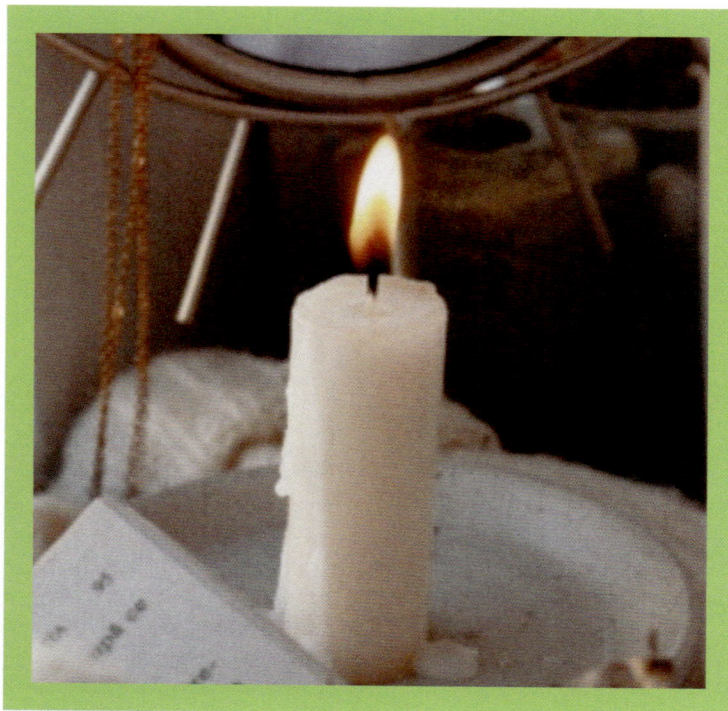

How Candles Burn

During Advent, many churches and homes have an Advent wreath. The Advent wreath has four candles for the four weeks of Advent. The Bible tells us, "The people who walked in darkness have seen a great light" (Isaiah 9:2). Who is this great light? The candles on the Advent wreath are a symbol of Jesus as the light of the world.

Have you ever wondered how candles burn? The fire needs oxygen and fuel. Candles can keep burning because the wick (the part of the candle you light) and the wax work together to make sure the fire has enough heat and fuel.

When you light the candle wick, it catches fire. The fire needs fuel to keep burning and the fire's heat melts the wax into liquid. Then the wax gets so hot that it turns into a gas. The fuel is the melted wax.

Do you notice that a candle gets smaller and smaller the longer you burn it? That's because the wax is being burned up by the flame. Once all the wax around the wick is melted, the candle will go out. Just like a car stops working when it runs out of gas, the candle will stop burning when it runs out of fuel from the wax.

What is the fuel that keeps a candle burning?

Advent

Behold, you will conceive in your womb and bear a son, and you shall name Him Jesus. He will be great and will be called the Son of the Most High.

-Luke 1:30-31

The Annunciation

Art by Sandro Botticelli (c. 1485–1492)

- What do you notice first in this painting?

- What do you think is happening here?

- Can you find small lines of shiny gold? Point to them. What do you think they represent?

lesson 16

The Annunciation

Advent is a time when we prepare to welcome baby Jesus. Today we will listen to the Scripture that tells us how Mary welcomed Jesus into the world and said "yes" to becoming the Mother of God. We will begin with a very special visitor who came to her with a message:

He said, "Hail, favored one! The Lord is with you." But she was greatly troubled at what was said and pondered what sort of greeting this might be.

Then the angel said to her, "Do not be afraid, Mary, for you have found favor with God. Behold, you will conceive in your womb and bear a son, and you shall name him Jesus. He will be great and will be called Son of the Most High, and the Lord God will give him the throne of David his father, and he will rule over the house of Jacob forever, and of his kingdom there will be no end."

Mary asked how this could be possible. And the angel said to her in reply:

"The Holy Spirit will come upon you, and the power of the Most High will overshadow you. Therefore, the child to be born will be called holy, the Son of God."

Mary said, "Behold, I am the handmaid of the Lord. May it be done to me according to your word." Then the angel departed from her. (Luke 1:28-38)

**What did you hear? Who visited Mary? What did he tell her?
Whose power will make this happen?
Who will her baby be? What will He be like? What is Mary's answer?
What are some ways you say "yes" to God like Mary did?**

Advent

lesson 16

About Doves

At the Annunciation, when Mary said "yes" to becoming the Mother of God, the angel Gabriel told her that the Holy Spirit would come to her. In the Bible, the dove is often a symbol of the Holy Spirit. What a special honor for such a small animal! People in Jesus' time were familiar with doves. Are you? Today we will learn a bit about them.

Doves can be found almost anywhere in the world. They can survive in deserts, mountains, and tropical forests. Though they are tough birds that can live in almost any environment, in the wild they only live about 3-5 years.

Doves eat mostly insects, seeds, nuts, and fruit. But if they live in captivity or places where people feed them, they will eat almost anything they are given. Doves also drink water differently than most birds. Usually, birds take some water in their beaks and tilt their head back so the water will slide down their throats. But doves suck water up through their beaks like a straw!

The sound doves make is not a tweet or a chirp but a soft "coo". Male doves make this sound mostly to attract female doves. Doves mate for life, so once the male attracts the female with his coo, they will stick together their whole lives.

What is one thing you learned about doves today?

RELIGION

lesson 16

Ancient of Days by William Blake (1794)

Baltimore Catechism

Question 11: Why can there be but one God?

Answer: There can be but one God, because God, being supreme and infinite, cannot have an equal.

lesson 17

The Meeting of Mary and Elisabeth

Art by Carl Heinrich Bloch (1866)

- How many people are in this painting? Count them.
- Can you find Mary's halo? Point to it.
- Mary is the person standing at the bottom of the stairs. Look at the white veil she is wearing. See how the artist made the veil look see-through? The artist did that by painting in <u>layers</u>. That means you paint something on the bottom first and then something different on top of it. First, the artist painted Mary and the stairs, and then he added a light layer of paint for the veil. Because he added white paint on top in only some places, it looks see-through! Point to the veil and tell me what you can see in the layer underneath it.

Advent

The Visitation

After the angel Gabriel appeared to Mary and she said "yes" to being the mother of Jesus, Mary went to visit her cousin Elizabeth. Elizabeth was pregnant too. The angel Gabriel also appeared to Elizabeth's husband, Zechariah! Gabriel told him they would have a son even though they were very old. Gabriel also said that Zechariah's son would be special, and that he would be filled with the Holy Spirit, even in his mother's womb.

Let's read the Scripture story to learn what happened when Mary visited Elizabeth:

> *During those days Mary set out and traveled to the hill country in haste to a town of Judah, where she entered the house of Zechariah and greeted Elizabeth.*
>
> *When Elizabeth heard Mary's greeting, the infant leaped in her womb, and Elizabeth, filled with the Holy Spirit, cried out in a loud voice and said, "Most blessed are you among women, and blessed is the fruit of your womb.*
>
> *And how does this happen to me, that the mother of my Lord should come to me?*
>
> *For at the moment the sound of your greeting reached my ears, the infant in my womb leaped for joy. Blessed are you who believed that what was spoken to you by the Lord would be fulfilled."* (Luke 1:39-45)

Let's read again what Elizabeth first said to Mary. Do those words sound familiar?

lesson 17

About Donkeys

Donkeys are mentioned many times in the Bible because lots of people used donkeys to travel. In Jesus' time, they did not have cars, so they would either ride on a donkey or put their belongings on the donkey's back. What a useful animal!

Donkeys are domesticated animals. Domesticated means they have been used by humans for so many years that they cannot live well in the wild. They must be taken care of by humans.

Donkeys are useful to humans because they are strong. A donkey can carry as much as a horse and can walk on rocky or uneven ground even better than a horse!

Donkeys eat a lot of hay each day to stay strong and healthy. But donkeys don't need much water. Of all the domesticated animals in the world, only the camel needs less water than a donkey. Donkeys are picky about their water. If they think their water is too dirty, they won't drink it!

What is one thing you learned about donkeys today?

Advent

The Trinity by Laurent Girardin (c. 1460)

Baltimore Catechism

Question 12: How many Persons are there in God?

Answer: In God there are three Divine Persons, really distinct, and equal in all things—the Father, the Son, and the Holy Ghost.

lesson 18

The Adoration of the Shepherds

Art by Agnolo Bronzino (1540)

- What do you notice first in this painting?

- What do you see in the foreground? What do you see in the background?

- Can you see the angel in the midground? What do you think it is doing?

- What story is this picture telling? Can you tell it to me?

lesson 18

The Birth of Jesus

The most important event that ever happened was when God became a man. But remember, Jesus didn't start out as a man. He started out as a baby, just like you! Before He was born, Mary and Joseph had to travel far from their home to Bethlehem. There was no place for them to stay in Bethlehem, so they had to sleep where the animals were kept. That is where Jesus was born.

On the night Jesus was born, an angel appeared to shepherds in a field. He told the shepherds:

> *"Do not be afraid; for behold, I proclaim to you good news of great joy that will be for all the people. For today in the city of David a savior has been born for you who is Messiah and Lord.*
>
> *And this will be a sign for you: you will find an infant wrapped in swaddling clothes and lying in a manger."* (Luke 2:10-12)

The shepherds were amazed and ran as fast as they could to meet Jesus. They were so happy to meet Him that they left praising God and told everyone what the angel said.

What stood out to you most about Jesus' birth?

How would you feel if you were one of the shepherds?

About Cows & Oxen

The Bible tells us that when Jesus was born, He was laid in a manger. A manger is a place where animals' food is kept. Mary and Joseph probably used a manger as Jesus' bed because of the soft hay inside.

Last week, we learned that donkeys eat lots of hay to stay healthy and strong. Some other animals that eat lots of hay are cows and oxen. Donkeys, cows, and oxen were all probably present when Jesus was born!

Just like the donkey, cows and oxen are domesticated animals. That means they are useful to humans and need humans to take care of them. Cows provide us milk. Most of the milk you find at the grocery store comes from cows. Cow's milk is also used to make cheese and butter. Cows are useful because we can eat their meat, called beef.

Oxen are a special type of male cattle used to pull heavy things. An ox is strong and dependable. It is one of the strongest animals in the world! When a person is super strong, you might hear someone say they are "as strong as an ox!" Oxen are used to pull wagons, to plow fields, and to do work on the farm that requires great strength.

What is one thing you learned about cows and oxen today?

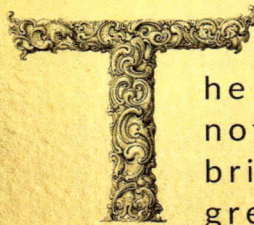The angel said to them, 'Do not be afraid; for behold, I bring you good news of great joy which will be for all the people; for today in the city of David there has been born for you a Savior, who is Christ the Lord. This will be a sign for you: you will find a baby wrapped in cloths and lying in a manger.'

-Luke 2:10-12

lesson 19

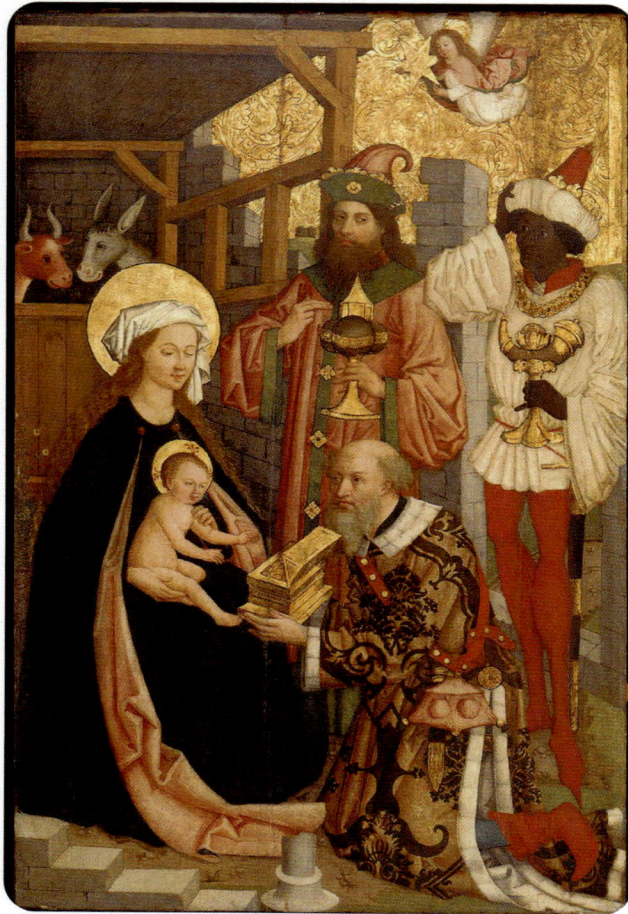

The Adoration of the Magi

Art by Bartholomäus Zeitblom (c. 1490–1505)

- What colors do you notice in this painting?

- Do you notice any shiny gold? Point to the places where you see gold.

- The Magi are often referred to as the Three Kings. What do you think the gold in this painting represents?

lesson 19

The Wise Men Visit Jesus

Christmas

We heard that after Jesus was born, shepherds came to visit Him. But they were not His only visitors! Today, we will hear about some visitors called the Magi (or Wise Men), who followed a guiding star to meet Jesus:

After Jesus was born in Bethlehem of Judea, wise men from the East came to Jerusalem, asking, "Where is the child who has been born king of the Jews? For we observed his star at its rising and have come to pay him homage."

When they were asked where the child would be born, the men said:

"In Bethlehem of Judea; for so it has been written by the prophet: 'And you, Bethlehem, in the land of Judah, are by no means least among the rulers of Judah; for from you shall come a ruler who is to shepherd my people Israel.'"

The Wise Men followed the star until it stopped, which is where they found Jesus! The Bible tells us:

When they saw that the star had stopped, they were overwhelmed with joy. On entering the house, they saw the child with Mary his mother; and they knelt down and paid him homage. Then, opening their treasure chests, they offered him gifts of gold, frankincense, and myrrh. (Matthew 2:1-2, 5-6, 9-11)

What did you hear?

What did the wise men do?

The wise men adored Jesus with their whole bodies.

I wonder how we can adore Jesus, too?

Let's Learn About Camels

The Bible tells us that the Magi came from the east, and they are often pictured traveling on camels as they followed the star to Jesus. Have you ever seen a camel? Today, we will learn about these amazing animals.

Not many animals can live in the desert, but the camel's body has adapted to help it survive in a hot, dry climate. Adapted means that an animal's body has developed special features that help it survive in certain places. One of the most important features that helps a camel survive in the desert is the hump on its back.

Camels have either one or two humps on their backs. Camels eat plants, but there are not many plants or sources of water in the desert. That's no problem for camels! Their humps store fat to give their bodies energy to walk for months without food and water.

In the desert, a lot of sand blows around, but the camel has long eyelashes to help keep sand out of its eyes. It also has thick pads on its feet so it can walk on the hot, uneven sand and not be harmed.

What is one thing you learned about camels today?

RELIGION

Christmas

God the Father by Jacob Herreyns I (18th century)

Baltimore Catechism

Question 13: Is the Father God?

Answer: The Father is God and the first Person of the Blessed Trinity.

lesson 20

Presentation of Christ at the Temple

Art by Giotto di Bondone (1306)

- What do you first notice in this image?

- How many figures do you see in this painting? Count them.

- This type of painting is called a <u>fresco</u>. Frescoes are paintings that are actually part of a wall or ceiling! They are made by taking wet plaster and mixing it with paint to make an image. The image then becomes part of the building. This painting is old, and the color is fading in some places. Do you see the gray wall where the color has started to fade?

- The man on the left is St. Joseph. What do you think he is holding?

lesson 20

Simeon and Anna Meet Jesus

Christmas

So far, we have read about the shepherds and the wise men, who were filled with joy when they met Jesus. Today, we will learn about two people who waited a long time to meet Jesus. Their names were Simeon and Anna. God promised them they would meet the Messiah, Jesus, and God always keeps His promises.

The Bible tells us that Mary and Joseph brought Jesus to the Temple one day when He was still a baby. Simeon was also at the Temple. The Bible tells us he was a holy man who loved God very much. The Holy Spirit told Simeon that before he died, he would meet the Messiah. When Simeon saw Jesus, he said:

> *"Lord, now let your servant go in peace, according to your word; for my eyes have seen your salvation which you have prepared in the presence of all peoples, a light for revelation to the Gentiles and for glory to your people Israel."* (Luke 2:29-32)

Mary and Joseph were amazed at what Simeon said! Anna was also at the Temple that day. She was old, and her husband had died many years before. She lived at the Temple and prayed day and night. The Bible tells us that when she saw Jesus, she gave thanks to God and spoke about the child to all who were awaiting the redemption of Jerusalem. (Luke 2:38)

What did you hear?
There could have been several babies brought to the Temple that day.
How did Simeon and Anna know who Jesus was?
What did Anna do after seeing this Promised One of God?

lesson 20

Animal Families

The Bible tells us that when Mary and Joseph presented Jesus in the Temple, they brought two turtledoves or pigeons as an offering. The law said pigeons OR turtledoves were acceptable because pigeons and doves are in the same family of birds.

When scientists talk about a family of animals, they don't just mean a mom, a dad, and their young. A family means animals that are different but share certain features. Pigeons and doves have different body types, but they are similar in many ways.

Look at the pictures below and match the animals in the same animal family. What makes them similar? What is different about them?

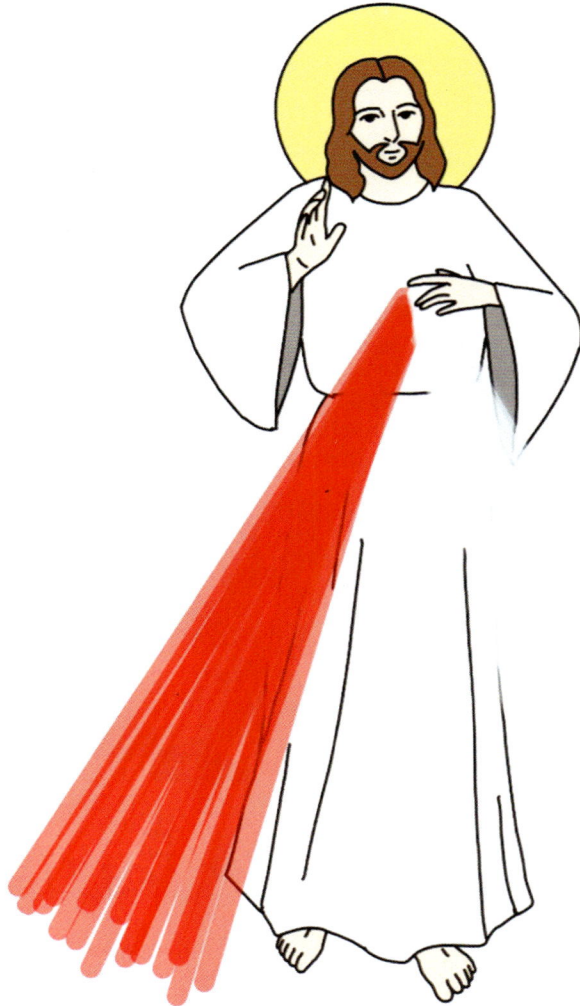

Baltimore Catechism

Question 14: Is the Son God?

Answer: The Son is God and the second Person of the Blessed Trinity.

Rest on the Flight into Egypt

Art by Luc-Olivier Merson (1879)

- What do you notice first in this painting?
- Do you think it is day or night? What makes you think that?
- Where do you see light? Can you find the fire?
- Tell me a story about what you see in this painting.

lesson 21

The Flight into Egypt

Not everyone was happy about the birth of Jesus. The Magi asked for directions from King Herod and told him they were looking for a king who was to be born in Bethlehem. Herod was a cruel king and did not like the idea of another king being born. He wanted to harm Jesus. But God knew of King Herod's evil plans and told Joseph how to protect Jesus and Mary. The Bible tells us:

An angel of the Lord appeared to Joseph in a dream and said, "Rise, take the child and his mother, and flee to Egypt, and remain there until I tell you . . ." And he rose and took the child and his mother by night and departed to Egypt and remained there until the death of Herod. This was to fulfill what the Lord had spoken by the prophet, "Out of Egypt I called my son." (Matthew 2:13-15)

What did you hear? Who visited Joseph? What did he tell Joseph to do?

How did Joseph answer? Who is this son of God?

SCIENCE

lesson 21

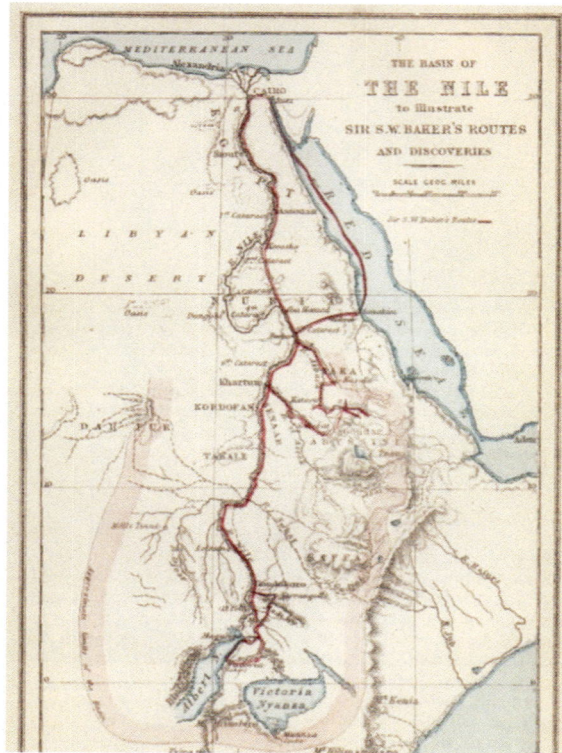

The Nile River

The Holy Family fled to Egypt, and while they were there, they probably saw one of Egypt's most important features—the Nile River. When most people think of the Nile River, they think of Egypt, but the Nile is more than four thousand miles long and travels through many countries in the continent of Africa.

Look toward the bottom of the map above. The lake at the bottom of the map is Lake Victoria. That is where the Nile River starts. The water then travels north for thousands of miles, through many different countries and climates. It flows through areas with tropical climates where it is warm and rainy and through deserts where it is hot and dry.

We already learned about fresh water and salt water and how the fresh water from rivers and lakes picks up salt and other minerals from rocks as it travels to the ocean. The Nile River empties into the Mediterranean Sea. Find the blue sea at the top of the map above. That is the Mediterranean Sea. All the salt and minerals that are gathered along the Nile get dumped into the Mediterranean Sea.

Point to Lake Victoria at the bottom of the map. Then use your finger to follow the Nile River up to the Mediterranean Sea at the top of the map.

84

KINDERGARTEN

Dove of the Holy Spirit by Gian Lorenzo Bernini (c. 1660)

Baltimore Catechism

Question 15: Is the Holy Ghost God?

Answer: The Holy Ghost is God and the third Person of the Blessed Trinity.

Ordinary Time

The Good Shepherd

Art by Bartolome Esteban Murillo (c. 1660)

- What do you see in this painting?

- What do you notice in the foreground? What do you notice in the background?

- What do you think the child in this painting is doing? What do you think he can feel with his hands and feet?

- Tell me a story about this painting.

lesson 22

Jesus Returns to Nazareth

The Holy Family lived in Egypt for some time until it was safe to return to their home. The Bible tells us:

> *They returned into Galilee, to their own city, Nazareth. The child grew and became strong, filled with wisdom; and the favor of God was upon him.* (Luke 2:39-40)

The town where Jesus grew up, Nazareth, was not a big city but a small town. It was a place nobody thought was important. But we know that God can take small things and make them great! Nazareth is the place where Jesus lived, played, learned, and grew up.

In Nazareth, Mary and Joseph taught Jesus how to read, do chores, and pray their family prayers. Joseph worked as a carpenter, and though they were poor, their home was filled with love. Mary and Joseph helped Jesus grow strong and wise by their example, and as a child, Jesus was always obedient and loving.

Name one way your life is similar to Jesus' childhood.

Name one way your life is different from Jesus' childhood.

What do you think it would have been like to be friends with Jesus when He was a child?

Rivers & Lakes in Jesus' Land

Are there rivers or lakes where you live? The Sea of Galilee and the Jordan River are two bodies of water near Nazareth, where Jesus grew up and spent a lot of time.

The first thing to know about the Sea of Galilee is that it is not really a sea! It is a freshwater lake so large that people began calling it the Sea of Galilee, and the name stuck. Another name for it is Lake Tiberias.

Because of how big the Sea of Galilee is, it can become dangerous to swim or boat in when it storms. The Bible tells us that Jesus and His friends were on a boat in the Sea of Galilee when a storm rolled in. His friends were afraid because the waves were so big, but Jesus told the storm to calm, and the storm obeyed.

The Jordan River is where Jesus was baptized by His cousin, John the Baptist. The Jordan River flows from the Sea of Galilee and travels south. It is more than 150 miles long and empties out into a lake called the Dead Sea. The Dead Sea is so salty that no plants or animals can live in it!

Can you name the river and lakes in Jesus' land that we learned about today?

lesson 22

he child grew and became strong, filled with wisdom; and the favor of God was upon him.

-Luke 2:40

lesson 23

Christ Disputing in the Temple

Art by Jacopo Tintoretto (c. 1545)

- What do you notice first in this painting?
- What type of building do you think this takes place in?
- How do the people in this painting feel? Why do you think that?
- Can you find Jesus in the center of the painting? Point to His halo.
- Tell me a story about this painting.

Finding of Jesus in the Temple

Worshipping God and keeping His commandments were important to the Holy Family. Just as we go to Mass every Sunday, the Holy Family traveled to Jerusalem every year for the feast of Passover. The Bible tells us about a time when something unusual happened on their trip to Jerusalem. The Bible says:

When he was twelve years old, they went up according to custom; and when the feast was ended, as they were returning, the boy Jesus stayed behind in Jerusalem.

Mary and Joseph went back to Jerusalem and looked for Jesus, but they could not find Him. But then:

After three days they found him in the temple, sitting among the teachers, listening to them and asking them questions; and all who heard him were amazed at his understanding and his answers. And when they saw him they were astonished; and his mother said to him, "Son, why have you treated us so? Behold, your father and I have been looking for you anxiously." And he said to them, "How is it that you sought me? Did you not know that I must be in my Father's house?" (Luke 2:42-43, 46-49)

What did you hear?

What do you think Jesus meant, that He must be in His Father's house?

Who was Jesus calling His Father?

Ordinary Time

Rivers & Lakes in My Land

We learned about the lakes and rivers in Jesus' land where He spent much of His time. Now, let's learn about the lakes and rivers near you! Look at a map of your neighborhood or town and find the nearest river. Now find the nearest lake.

You may wonder: Where do rivers start? How do lakes form? The answer is that all rivers and lakes start at some high point like a mountain or a hill. The river or lake forms when rain or snowmelt flows down a mountain or from a spring whose water runs down a hill. Gravity makes the water flow down the mountain or hill, and if there is enough water it will form a river.

If the water from the river flows over soft rock, it will wear away the rock and eventually form a bowl or basin in the earth. Water from the river fills this basin, forming a lake. The water from the lake will usually continue flowing down a river until eventually the river empties out into the ocean. Remember, the water from rivers eventually ends up flowing to the ocean.

Find a river close to your home. Then look at an atlas or online map and find where your river begins. Does it begin on a mountain? In a lake? At another river?

Find where your river ends (where it meets up with another river, lake, or the ocean).

lesson 23

The Holy Trinity, from Via Felicitatis by Hans Schäufelein (1513)

Baltimore Catechism

Question 16: What is the Blessed Trinity?

Answer: The Blessed Trinity is one God in three Divine Persons.

lesson 24

The Baptism of Christ

Art by Antoine Coypel (c. 1690)

- What colors do you see in this painting?

- What do you think is happening here?

- The Holy Spirit is often depicted as a dove. Can you find the dove in this painting?

- The artist uses light and shadow in this painting. Where is the light coming from? Point to the places where you see light. Point to the places where you see shadow.

lesson 24

The Baptism of the Lord

We read about when Mary visited her cousin Elizabeth, and the baby in Elizabeth's womb leaped for joy at Mary's voice. That baby grew up to be John the Baptist. He was holy and wanted everyone to love and follow God. People from all over would come to the Jordan River to be baptized by John. Today, we will hear about the day Jesus came to see John the Baptist at the Jordan River. The Bible tells us:

Then Jesus came from Galilee to the Jordan to John, to be baptized by him. John would have prevented him, saying, "I need to be baptized by you, and do you come to me?" But Jesus answered him, "Let it be so now; for thus it is fitting for us to fulfill all righteousness." Then he consented.

And when Jesus was baptized, he went up immediately from the water, and behold, the heavens were opened and he saw the Spirit of God descending like a dove and alighting on him; and lo, a voice from heaven, saying, "This is my beloved Son, with whom I am well pleased." (Matthew 3:13-17)

What did you hear?
Did John want to baptize Jesus at first?
What happened when Jesus was baptized?
What would you do if you were there when Jesus was baptized and saw this happen?

The Jordan River

The Jordan River is important in Jesus' land. Many Christians visit it every year to see the place where Jesus was baptized. Let's learn more about the Jordan River today!

We learned that all rivers begin at a high point, like a mountain or hill, and then flow downward to a low point, like the ocean. The Jordan River begins at Mount Hermon, which is the highest point in Israel. From there, it flows south until it reaches the Sea of Galilee. Remember the Sea of Galilee is not really a sea but a large freshwater lake.

From the Sea of Galilee, the Jordan River flows south until it empties into the Dead Sea. Remember that the Dead Sea got its name because it is so salty that no plants or animals can live in it. The Dead Sea is also a lake, but it is a salt lake, which means it is a lake that has salt water. That is unusual—there are only thirty salt lakes in the whole world! The Dead Sea is so salty because it is the lowest point of land on Earth. All the salt and sediment the Jordan River picks up along its path gets dumped into the Dead Sea. But, there is not a lot of space for all that salt, and the water has nowhere else to go. All that salt builds up and makes the Dead Sea ten times saltier than the ocean!

Can you tell me two of the lakes (or seas) that the Jordan River flows into?

Which one is a freshwater lake? Which one is a saltwater lake?

Baltimore Catechism

Question 17: Are the three Divine Persons one and the same God?

Answer: The three Divine Persons are one and the same God, having one and the same Divine nature.

The Angelus

Art by Jean-François Millet (c. 1858)

- What colors do you see in this painting?

- What time of day do you think it is? What makes you think that?

- What do you see in the foreground? What do you see in the background?

- What are the people in this painting doing?

- The style of this painting is called realism. Realist painters often paint nature or ordinary parts of daily life and try to show them just as they are. Does anything in this painting look the way it looks in real life? Point to it.

lesson 25

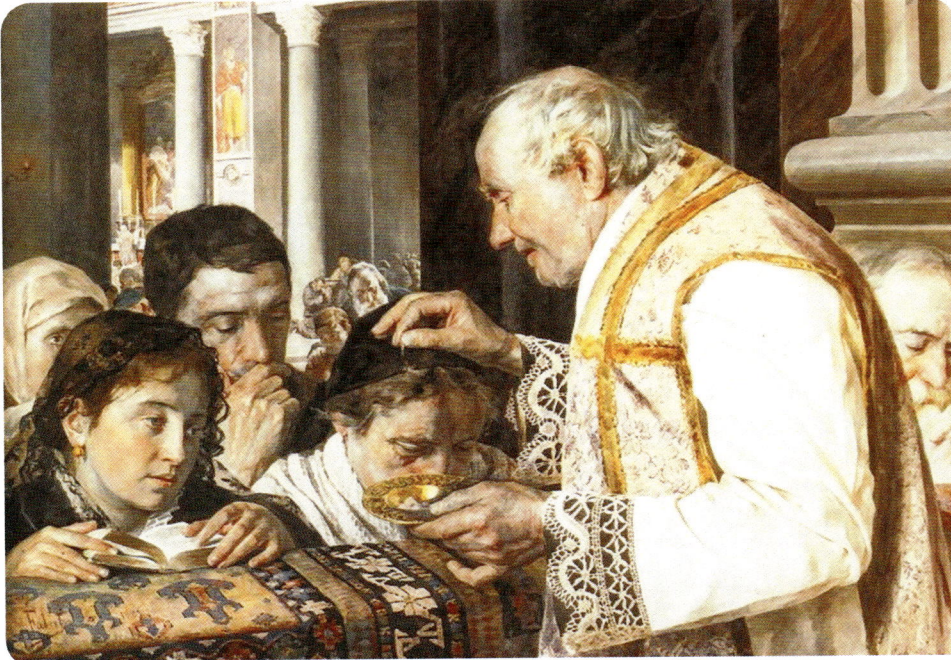

Let's Learn About Lent

Popielec (Ash Wednesday) by Julian Fałat (1881)

We have experienced three liturgical seasons—Ordinary Time, Advent, and Christmas—and now we are beginning a new liturgical season: Lent! Remember that each liturgical season has a color that goes with it. Green is for growing, purple is for preparation, and gold and white are for celebration.

During Lent, you will see the priest at Mass wearing purple because Lent is a season of preparation. What are we preparing for? We are preparing for Easter, when we will celebrate Jesus' rising from the dead! His life is stronger than death!

How can we prepare our hearts for Easter, the Feast of Feasts? By thinking about God's love for us in a different way. During Lent, we think about God's love for us when He died on the Cross. Jesus loves us so much He laid down His life for us and took it up again. During Lent, we do specific things to show God our love.

Prayer: During Lent, we pray more. We listen to God. We talk to God to tell Him we love Him. We thank Him for the gifts He has given us.

Fasting: During Lent, we choose something good to "lay down" so we can be more like the Good Shepherd who laid down His life for us. In this way, we make more room for God in our lives.

Almsgiving: We can show God our love by showing love to others! During Lent, we give our time, talent, and treasure to show God's love to others.

> **How can you show God your love by prayer, fasting, and almsgiving this Lent?**

Lent

How Ashes Are Made

The first day of Lent is Ash Wednesday. It is called Ash Wednesday because during Mass we receive ashes on our forehead. Ashes are a reminder that we must focus on loving God and spending time with Him and not on the things of this world. Today we are going to learn how ash is made!

Fire always needs something to burn, just like you need food to stay strong and healthy. Wood, paper, and plants are good fuel for fire. When they burn, some of what is in them turns to gas and smoke but not everything. The fire burns what it can use for fuel, and what it can't use as fuel turns to ash. You can usually find ash in fireplaces or firepits. It looks like a gray powder.

For Ash Wednesday, we take palm branches from last year's Palm Sunday Mass and burn them until only ashes remain. Those ashes are mixed with holy water or blessed oil so they become thick and will stick on your forehead. We receive ashes on our foreheads in the shape of a cross as a sign that we love God and that God loves us.

What is one thing you learned about ashes today?

Baltimore Catechism

Question 18: Which are the chief creatures of God?

Answer: The chief creatures of God are men and angels.

lesson 26

Elijah in the Desert

Art by Washington Allston (1818)

- What do you notice first in this painting?
- What do you see in the foreground? What do you see in the background?
- Can you find water in this painting? Point to it.
- Can you find a person in this painting? Point to him.
- What would it feel like to be in this wilderness? What sounds might you hear?

lesson 26

40 Days in the Wilderness

After His Baptism and before Jesus began to teach people about God's love, He took time to prepare. He went into the wilderness for forty days and forty nights. There was not much food in the wilderness, and Jesus had a difficult time. The Bible tells us:

> *The Spirit immediately drove him out into the wilderness. And he was in the wilderness forty days, tempted by Satan; and he was with the wild beasts; and the angels ministered to him.* (Mark 1:12)

His time in the wilderness gave Jesus more time to pray. He was able to let go of all the things of the world to make space for prayer and preparation. It was hard to do, but it made Jesus stronger and ready for His mission.

The forty days of Lent are like Jesus' forty days in the wilderness. We use this season to prepare for Easter, making time in our day for prayer and space in our hearts for God's love. Just like Jesus did!

What did you hear?

How do you think Jesus felt in the wilderness?

How can we make time in our day for prayer and space in our hearts for God's love during Lent?

Wilderness in the Holy Land

The wilderness in the Holy Land is called the Judean Wilderness. The Bible mentions it several times. King David and the prophet Elijah both fled to the wilderness to escape their enemies. John the Baptist preached in the wilderness. And Jesus went into the wilderness for forty days and forty nights to prepare for His ministry. Today we will learn about what this Judean Wilderness is like.

The Judean Wilderness is also called the Judean Desert because it is a rock desert. The ground is rocky, and there are many cliffs, caves, and canyons. Because there is so much rock and so little rain, it is difficult to grow food there.

When you think of a desert, you might think of a place with lots of sand and no water. But the Judean Desert does have some water, mostly in the winter when it rains. The rain collects in wadis, riverbeds that are usually dry but fill up and become streams and rivers when it rains.

Because it can be hot during the day, many animals in the Judean Desert are nocturnal. Nocturnal means they sleep during the day and are awake at night. The Arabian leopard, the Desert Lynx, and the sand dune cat all live in the Judean Desert. It is easier for them to hunt when it is dark because they can hide from their prey. And since they sleep during the day when it is hot, they are more comfortable in the cooler air of night.

What is one thing you learned about the Judean Desert today?

lesson 26

Lent

One doesn't live on bread alone, but every word that comes forth from the mouth of God.

-Matthew 4:4

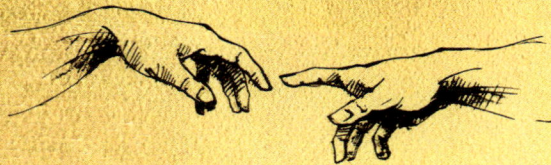

lesson 27

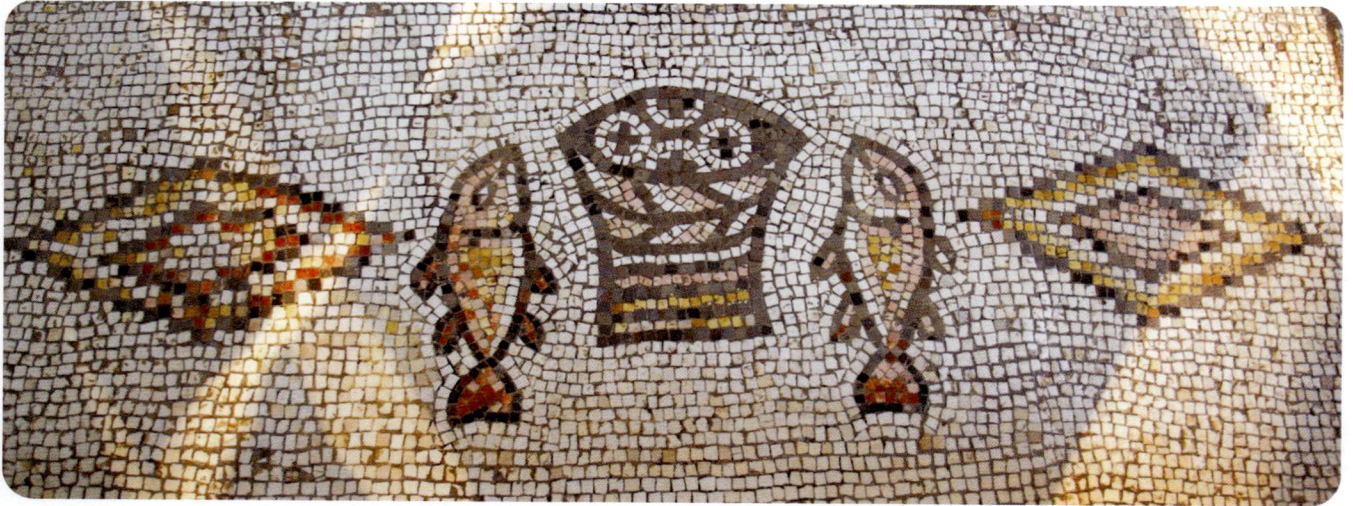

Loaves & Fishes Mosaic of Tabgha

Artist Unknown (c. 300)

- What do you see?

- What shapes can you find in this artwork?

- This type of art is called a mosaic. A mosaic is made by taking small pieces of material and putting them together to make an image. Can you see the square tiles that make up this mosaic? Point to the tiles that are different colors.

- This mosaic is found on the floor of a church, near where Jesus fed five thousand people with only a few loaves of bread and some fish. If you were to make a mosaic on the floor of your home, what image would you make?

lesson 27

Feeding the Five Thousand

Let's remember the parable of the mustard seed. Jesus said that even though it is one of the smallest seeds, it can grow into one of the largest trees. Let's think about that parable as we learn about a time when Jesus took a little food and used it to feed a large crowd of five thousand people! The Bible tells us:

As he landed he saw a great crowd, and he had compassion on them, because they were like sheep without a shepherd; and he began to teach them many things. And when it grew late, his disciples came to him and said, "This is a lonely place, and the hour is now late; send them away, to go into the country and villages round about and buy themselves something to eat."

Jesus told His friends they should feed the crowd. They went around to find food, but all they could find was five loaves of bread and two fish. They wondered how this could feed five thousand people! But Jesus was not worried.

Taking the five loaves and the two fish he looked up to heaven, and blessed and broke the loaves, and gave them to the disciples to set before the people; and he divided the two fish among them all. And they all ate and were satisfied. (Mark 6:34-44)

What did you hear?
What does this Scripture teach us about Jesus?
What does Jesus want us to know about who He is?

Wilderness Where You Live

Jesus spent forty days and forty nights in the Judean Wilderness. We learned what the wilderness near Him was like, but what is the wilderness like near you? Wilderness is an area where no humans live and nature lies mostly untouched. Think about the land outside your town or city—what does it look like?

There are many types of wildernesses. Which one of these is near you?

Forest: Forests are large areas covered mostly by trees. Streams or rivers often run through them.

Desert: Deserts are hot, dry areas that get very little rain. Not many plants can grow there due to these conditions. Deserts can be sandy or rocky.

Swamp: Swamps are forests flooded with water. They are an in-between kind of wilderness—not totally land but not totally water.

Mountain: Mountains are parts of the earth that stretch up high. The tops of mountains are usually rocky and are often snow-covered in the winter. Many mountains are connected to other mountains in a line. This is called a mountain range.

Meadow: A meadow is a large area covered in grass. Animals like cows or sheep often graze in meadows. In the spring and summer, you can often find wildflowers growing in the grass, too.

What is the wilderness like near you?
Does the wilderness look different in the summer and winter? What is the difference?

lesson 27

The Heavenly Hosts by Gustave Doré (c. 1866)

Baltimore Catechism

Question 19: What are angels?

Answer: Angels are bodiless spirits created to adore and enjoy God in heaven.

lesson 28

Christ's Entry into Jerusalem

Art by Albrecht Dürer (1510)

- This type of art is called a <u>woodcut print</u>. It was made by making cuts in a block of wood to form a picture. It was then used like a stamp! Have you ever used a stamp?

- What is the first thing you notice about this artwork?

- What do you think is happening?

lesson 28

Palm Sunday

When Jesus was young, the Holy Family went to Jerusalem each year to celebrate the feast of Passover. You already heard about when Jesus was twelve years old and stayed in the Temple after Passover to discuss Scripture. Let's read about what happened when Jesus came to Jerusalem for Passover as an adult with His closest friends:

When the great crowd that had come to the feast heard that Jesus was coming to Jerusalem, they took palm branches and went out to meet him and cried out: "Hosanna! Blessed is he who comes in the name of the Lord, the king of Israel." (John 12:12-13)

What did you hear?

Why do you think the people treated Jesus this way?

What would you do if you heard that Jesus was coming to your town?

About Palm Trees

We read that when Jesus entered Jerusalem, people in the crowd took palm branches to go out and meet Him. They waved the palms and laid them on the ground before Jesus to give Him a royal welcome. At Mass on Palm Sunday, we get palm branches to remember the way the crowd welcomed and honored Jesus. Today, we will learn about where these palm branches come from.

Palm branches come from palm trees, which are usually found in places where it is warm all year round. Even though we call them palm trees, they are not actually trees at all! They are woody plants closer to bamboo or grass than an actual tree. But when a palm plant's stem grows tall, it looks like a tree.

Palm trees are evergreen, which means they do not lose their leaves in the autumn and winter. Their leaves are called fronds, which are long and thin and spread out along the branch.

The coconut fruit grows on palm trees, but not all palm trees can grow coconuts. Only one type of palm tree can produce coconuts, and they are usually found in tropical areas near the ocean.

What is one thing you learned about palm trees today?

lesson 28

Baltimore Catechism

Question 20: Who were the first man and woman?

Answer: The first man and woman were Adam and Eve.

The Last Supper

Art by Leonardo da Vinci (1498)

- What do you notice first in this artwork?

- What do you think is happening?

- How many windows do you see? Point to them. What do you think the three windows represent?

- Everyone is sitting at a table. What meal do you think they are eating—breakfast, lunch, or dinner? Tell me what you think they are having at this meal.

Lent

The Last Supper

The feast of Passover was important for Jesus' family and friends. They celebrated God freeing their people from slavery in Egypt. When God freed the Israelites from Egypt, He told them to have a meal of lamb, unleavened bread, and bitter herbs. He also told them to take blood from the lamb they were eating and put it on the door. Doing so would be a sign of the covenant (which is a special promise) that they were God's friends.

Every year to remember Passover, Jesus' family and friends had a meal of lamb, bread with no leavening, and bitter herbs, just as God commanded them. Let's read about the last Passover Jesus celebrated, when something special happened:

He took bread, and when he had given thanks, he broke it and gave it to them, saying, "This is my body, which is given for you. Do this in remembrance of me." And likewise the cup after they had eaten, saying, "This cup is the new covenant in my blood, which will be shed for you." (Luke 22:19-20)

What did you hear?
Do Jesus' words sound familiar?

About Bitter Foods

For Passover, Jesus and His friends ate lamb, unleavened bread, and bitter herbs. We already learned about lambs and sheep and how important they were for food in Jesus' land. We also learned that leavening creates air bubbles that make bread rise. Unleavened bread is bread with no leavening, which means it is a flat bread. Wow! You already know so much about the Passover foods Jesus ate! But what about those bitter herbs? Today we will learn what makes things bitter.

Think about the foods you eat. They don't all taste the same, do they? That is because your tongue has taste buds, special bumps that tell your body whether food has certain flavors. Your taste buds and your nose are a tasting team. When you bite into food, the food releases chemicals that travel up to your nose. Your nose and your taste buds work together to tell you what that food tastes like!

There are five flavors your taste buds can detect: sweet, salty, sour, savory, and bitter. Sweet foods have sugars in them, like chocolate or berries. Salty foods have salt in or on them, like potato chips or popcorn. Sour foods have acids in them, like lemon or pickles. Savory foods have an earthy taste to them, like meat or mushrooms.

Bitter foods can have a taste that does not seem very good at first. Fortunately, we can cook green vegetables and other bitter foods to make them delicious!

What is one thing you learned about taste and bitter foods today?

What is your favorite taste: sweet, salty, sour, savory, or bitter?

lesson 29

The Expulsion of Adam and Eve from Paradise
by Benjamin West (1791)

Baltimore Catechism

Question 21: What is the sin called which we inherit from our first parents?

Answer: The sin which we inherit from our first parents is called original sin.

The Crucifixion

Art by Francisco de Zurbarán (1627)

- What do you notice first about this painting?

- Notice the light and shadow in this painting. What side does the light seem to be coming from?

- Do you see anything on the Cross? Point to what you see.

- What looks real in this painting?

- What looks not real about this painting?

- How does this painting make you feel?

lesson 30

The Passion of Jesus

The Three Crosses by Rembrandt (1653)

Last week, we heard Jesus tell His friends, "This is My body, which is given for you." That is what He said at the Last Supper on Holy Thursday, when He gave us His body and blood in the Eucharist.

On Good Friday, Jesus showed His love for us by sacrificing His body on the Cross. He loves us so much that He gave His whole life for us. By giving His body on the Cross, Jesus opened up heaven for everyone who wants to be His friend.

When Jesus was on the Cross, there was a thief named Dismas. Dismas saw Jesus' great love on the Cross and wanted to be His friend. Dismas told Jesus:

> *"Jesus, remember me when you come into your kingdom." [Jesus] replied to him, "Amen, I say to you, today you will be with me in Paradise."* (Luke 23:42-43)

Today, we know that man as St. Dismas because he is in heaven with Jesus!

What did you hear?
How do you think Dismas felt when Jesus told him he would be with Jesus in heaven?
What do you think Jesus' sacrifice shows us about His love?

Lent

About Vinegar

When Jesus was on the Cross and became thirsty, He was given vinegar to drink. Vinegar is a sour liquid, so the drink Jesus was given probably tasted sour. But vinegar was a useful liquid in Jesus' time, and we still use it today!

Vinegar is made by taking juice from grapes, apples, barley, or other foods. Then yeast is added to the juice. The juice has sugar in it, and yeast loves sugar! The yeast gobbles up the sugar and changes the sugar into alcohol. This process of turning sugar into alcohol is called <u>fermentation</u>.

After the fermentation process, there are tiny, living organisms called bacteria in the liquid. When oxygen (which is in the air) mixes with the liquid, the bacteria changes the alcohol into a strong smelling acid. The acid is what gives vinegar a sour taste.

Even though it is pretty stinky, vinegar is a useful liquid! We use it to flavor foods (like ketchup or salad dressing), to preserve foods and keep them from going bad (like pickles or fish), and to get rid of dirt and germs.

What is one thing you learned about vinegar today?

lesson 30

The Immaculate Conception of Los Venerables
by Bartolomé Esteban Murillo (c. 1680)

Baltimore Catechism

Question 22: Was any one ever preserved from original sin?

Answer: The Blessed Virgin Mary, through the merit of her Divine Son, was preserved free from the guilt of original sin, and this privilege is called her Immaculate Conception.

Lent

lesson 31

Resurrection

Art by Andrea Mantegna (1459)

- Describe the colors in this painting.
- How many figures are in this artwork? Count them.
- What area of the painting did the artist emphasize? How did he do that?
- What story is this painting telling?
- Close your eyes and tell me what you remember about the painting.

Easter

The Easter Miracle

After Jesus died on the Cross, His body was laid in a tomb. The tomb was a cave with a large stone rolled in front of the entrance. Let's read about what happened at the tomb on Easter Sunday:

After the sabbath, as the first day of the week was dawning, Mary Magdalene and the other Mary came to see the tomb. And behold, there was a great earthquake; for an angel of the Lord descended from heaven, approached, rolled back the stone, and sat upon it.

His appearance was like lightning and his clothing was white as snow. The guards were shaken with fear of him and became like dead men.

Then the angel said to the women in reply, "Do not be afraid! I know that you are seeking Jesus the crucified. He is not here, for he has been raised just as he said. Come and see the place where he lay. Then go quickly and tell his disciples, 'He has been raised from the dead, and he is going before you to Galilee; there you will see him.' Behold, I have told you."

Then they went away quickly from the tomb, fearful yet overjoyed, and ran to announce this to his disciples. And behold, Jesus met them on their way and greeted them. They approached, embraced his feet, and did him homage.

Then Jesus said to them, "Do not be afraid. Go tell my brothers to go to Galilee, and there they will see me." (Matthew 28:1-10)

What did you hear?
Who went to the tomb? Why? Who appeared to the women?
Have we heard these first words of the angel before?
What Good News did the angel of the Lord tell them? How did the women respond?

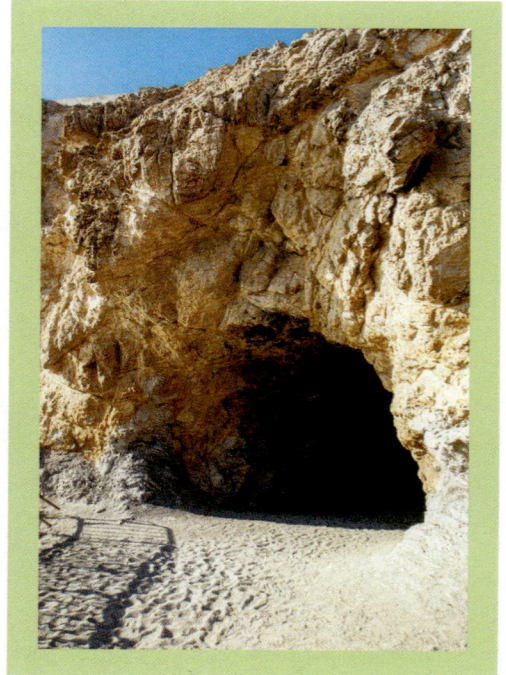

About Caves

After He died on the Cross, Jesus' body was placed in a cave used as a tomb. Today, we will learn about caves—how they are made and what they look like inside!

Caves are <u>hollow</u> spaces in the ground with openings large enough for humans to enter. Hollow means an empty place with only air, not something solid. So, caves are spaces in the ground where instead of earth and rock, there is empty space.

Often this empty space is created by flowing water underground and acid that eats the rock. Most caves are extremely dark unless they have large openings or cracks that let sunlight in.

Caves can form underground or in the sides of hills and cliffs. They can be tiny passages that humans can barely squeeze through or giant passages with different "rooms" that connect underground. Water will often drip through the cracks in a cave. The minerals from this water can build up into formations called <u>stalactites</u> and <u>stalagmites</u>. Stalactites form on the ceiling of a cave, and stalagmites form on the ground, usually right beneath stalactites.

What is one thing you learned about caves today?

Easter

Then the angel said to the women in reply, "Do not be afraid! I know that you are seeking Jesus the crucified. He is not here, for he has been raised just as he said."

-Matthew 28:5-6

lesson 32

Adoration of the Lamb

Art by Michiel Coxie (1558)

- Where does your eye go first in this painting?

- What do you see in the foreground? In the midground? In the background?

- What words would you use to describe the people in this artwork?

- Can you find the Holy Spirit (represented by a dove)?

- What story do you think this painting is telling?

Easter

Celebrating the Easter Season

We have spent the past few weeks in the season of Lent, preparing our hearts for Easter. Today, let's learn about the Easter season and how we celebrate Jesus' Resurrection!

Remember that every liturgical season has a special liturgical color to go along with it. Green is for growth, purple is for preparation, white and gold is for celebration. Easter is a time for celebration, so the liturgical colors for Easter are white and gold.

White and gold are the colors of light, and Easter is a time when we celebrate the light of the Risen Christ. Just as light is stronger than darkness, Jesus' life is stronger than death. We are given the light of Jesus at our baptism, and we celebrate our new life with Him during Easter.

The Easter season lasts seven weeks, and there are many ways to celebrate. At Mass, you may notice white and gold vestments, the lit Easter candle by the baptismal font, and singing "Alleluia!" once again. There are many signs and symbols of light and new life because Jesus is risen!

Think about ways your family can shine the light of the Risen Christ and keep the joy of Easter Sunday throughout the Easter season.

How does your family celebrate Easter?

How can you show joy during this Easter season?

What are some ways you can share the joy of Jesus' light and love?

Sunshine Brings Springtime

The liturgical season of Easter is a time of light and life. It always falls in the season of spring. Spring is also a season of light and new life. Today, we'll learn about springtime and how the sun plays a big role in the changing of the seasons.

The four seasons are: spring, summer, autumn, and winter. There are lots of differences between the seasons, and they all have to do with the sun. Our Earth moves around the sun in an orbit, a path that it always takes to travel around the sun. It takes Earth one year to go around the sun once.

When Earth moves around the sun, it is not straight up and down, but tilted. That means that as it moves in its orbit, some parts of Earth are tilted toward the sun at some points and away from the sun at other points. We call those different points the seasons.

Winter is when our part of Earth is tilted away from the sun. There is not much light and warmth because there is not much sunlight. The days are short, and few plants grow. But as Earth continues to move in its orbit, our part of Earth gets more and more sunlight. The days get longer, and the extra sunlight helps plants grow. Baby animals are often born as the weather gets warmer. We know it is the season of spring because light and life spring up to drive away the dark of winter!

What is one thing you learned about spring and the seasons today?

lesson 32

The Harrowing of Hell by an Anonymous Artist (11ᵗʰ century)

Baltimore Catechism

Question 23: Did God abandon man after he fell into sin?

Answer: God did not abandon man after he fell into sin, but promised him a Redeemer, who was to satisfy for man's sin and reopen to him the gates of heaven.

lesson 33

Road to Emmaus

Art by Robert Zünd (1877)

- What do you notice first in this painting?

- What do you see in the midground? What do you see in the background?

- Where do you think the people in this painting are going? Where do you think they are coming from?

- Imagine you are one of the people walking with Jesus. What do you think Jesus is saying? What would you talk about with Jesus?

Easter

The Road to Emmaus

On Easter Sunday, two of Jesus' friends were walking from Jerusalem to a town called Emmaus. They were sad because they knew that Jesus was not in the tomb, but they didn't know where He was. They didn't know He had risen from the dead.

As they were walking to Emmaus, they met a man along the way who explained to them that Jesus was the Savior that God had promised. He showed them that Scripture said all along this is what would happen. The disciples were amazed this man was so wise. They invited him to have dinner with them. Then, something amazing happened:

While he was with them at table, he took bread, said the blessing, broke it, and gave it to them. With that their eyes were opened and they recognized him, but he vanished from their sight.

Then they said to each other, "Were not our hearts burning [within us] while he spoke to us on the way and opened the scriptures to us?"

The disciples were so excited that they rushed back to Jerusalem to find Jesus' friends.

The two recounted what had taken place on the way and how he was made known to them in the breaking of the bread. (Luke 24:30-32, 35)

What did you hear?

Did any of the words sound familiar to you?

How would you feel if you were one of those friends?

Telling Time with the Sun

There are many ways we can tell time. One of the first ways is by figuring out whether it is day or night. Let's think of some differences between day and night. During the day, it is lighter outside, and we can see better. It is also usually warmer during the day than it is at night. Today, let's learn about what makes day and night, and why daytime brings light and heat and nighttime is dark and cold.

The difference between day and night is the location of the sun. Have you ever noticed that the sun seems like it is moving across the sky over the course of the day? The sun is not actually moving. Even though you can't feel it, the Earth is the one spinning and also circling the sun throughout the year.

Stand up and face me. Now, slowly spin around in place one time until you are facing me again. The Earth spins like that once every day! Now, imagine I am the sun and you are the Earth. If you see me, you are getting light and heat from the sun. That is day. Now slowly spin around, moving your head with the rest of your body. If you can't see me, that means your part of Earth isn't getting much light and heat from the sun. That is night.

The day has more light and warmth because that is the time our part of Earth is facing the sun. Since light and warmth come from the sun, at night when our part of Earth is facing away from the sun, it is dark and colder.

What are some things you now know about day and night?

Easter

Jesus as the Good Shepherd by Bernhard Plockhorst (1878)

Baltimore Catechism

Question 24: Who is the Redeemer?

Answer: Our Blessed Lord and Saviour Jesus Christ is the Redeemer of mankind.

The Ascension

Art by John Singleton Copley (1775)

- What colors do you see in this painting?

- Where do your eyes go first when you look at it? Why do you think that is?

- What are the people in this painting doing? How do you think they are feeling?

- Close your eyes and tell me what you remember about this painting.

lesson 34

Easter

The Ascension of Jesus into Heaven

After Jesus' resurrection, He showed Himself to many people and proved that He was indeed alive! For forty days, He stayed with His friends, teaching them about the Kingdom of God. He even ate breakfast with them! Then He told His friends to stay in Jerusalem and that He would send the Holy Spirit to help them. He said:

"You will receive power when the Holy Spirit comes upon you, and you will be my witnesses in Jerusalem, throughout Judea and Samaria, and to the ends of the earth."

When he had said this, as they were looking on, he was lifted up, and a cloud took him from their sight. While they were looking intently at the sky as he was going, suddenly two men dressed in white garments stood beside them. They said, "Men of Galilee, why are you standing there looking at the sky? This Jesus who has been taken up from you into heaven will return in the same way as you have seen him going into heaven." (Acts 1:9-11)

What did you hear?
What did Jesus' friends do when they saw Him being lifted up?
Who do you think the men dressed in white garments were?
What do you think this tells us about God's kingdom?

The Four Seasons and the Sun

The four seasons are spring, summer, autumn, and winter. We learned that the differences in the seasons are caused by whether our part of the Earth is tilting toward the sun. Today let's take a look at the different seasons!

Summer: When our part of Earth is tilting toward the sun, we are in the season of summer. The days are hot and long because our part of Earth is getting lots of light and heat from the sun. Warmth and sunlight encourage plants to grow. Many animals are out and about in the summer.

Autumn: As our part of Earth begins to tilt away from the sun, the days get shorter and cooler. This is the season of autumn. There is less light and heat from the sun, which causes tree leaves to change color and fall. Less sunlight means fewer plants can grow. Animals start getting ready for winter.

Winter: When our part of the Earth is tilted away from the sun, we experience the season of winter. The days are short and cold because there is little light and heat from the sun. Few plants can grow. Many animals go into a deep sleep during the winter. This is called <u>hibernation</u>.

Spring: As our part of Earth begins to tilt toward the sun, the days get longer and warmer. Plants begin to grow, and leaves return to trees. Animals come out from their winter homes, and new animals are born.

What did you learn about the seasons today?
What is your favorite season?

The Transfiguration with Christ flanked by two saints and with the Apostles below
by Cherubino Alberti (c. 1570-1615)

Baltimore Catechism

Question 25: What do you believe of Jesus Christ?

Answer: I believe that Jesus Christ is the Son of God, the second Person of the Blessed Trinity, true God and true man.

lesson 35

Pentecost

Art by El Greco (c. 1600)

- What do you notice first in this artwork?

- Where are the people looking?

- Can you find a dove in this artwork? What do you think it represents?

- Notice the light and shadow. Where is the light coming from?

- Close your eyes. Now, tell me what you remember about this artwork.

HISTORY

lesson 35

Pentecost: The Sending of the Holy Spirit

We heard in the last history lesson that before Jesus ascended into heaven He promised His friends that He would send the Holy Spirit to help them. Let's read what happened ten days after Jesus ascended into heaven:

When the time for Pentecost was fulfilled, they were all in one place together. And suddenly there came from the sky a noise like a strong driving wind, and it filled the entire house in which they were.
Then there appeared to them tongues as of fire, which parted and came to rest on each one of them.
And they were all filled with the holy Spirit and began to speak in different tongues, as the Spirit enabled them to proclaim. (Acts 2:1-4)

What did it look and sound like when the Holy Spirit came to Mary and the apostles?

What does fire do? What happens if I place water over fire?

What happens if I light a small fire in a dark room? If I am cold and stand near a fire, what does the fire do?

Fire changes. Fire transforms. What happened to Jesus' friends when the fire of the Holy Spirit descended upon them? How?

What then were they able to do once their fear transformed into love and passion? Can this same Holy Spirit transform us?

The Compass and Cardinal Directions

When you are reading a map, knowing the cardinal directions helps you know how to get from one place to another. The four cardinal directions are north, east, south, and west. The word cardinal means the basic, or most important. So north, east, south, and west are the most important directions to know.

North always points toward the North Pole at the top of the world. South always points to the South Pole at the bottom of the world. East is always the direction that the sun rises each morning. And west is always the direction the sun sets each evening.

When you look at a map, knowing the cardinal directions can help you see where different places are and how to get there. But to know where to go next, you need to know which direction you are facing. One way to know the direction you are facing is by using a compass.

A compass is a tool for finding direction. It has a magnetic needle that always points north. Magnets are pieces of metal that can pull other metals toward themselves or push those metals away. The needle on the compass is a magnet that is pulled toward Earth's magnetic north, so it will always point north.

Hikers, sailors, and pilots often use compasses to figure out which direction they are going. Directions are important for travelers, and a compass is a useful tool for finding directions!

What are the four cardinal directions?
What is a tool that helps you find directions?

Easter

The Ascension of Christ by Benvenuto Tisi (1520)

Let's review the questions from the Baltimore Catechism that have been covered so far.

lesson 36

Commodilla Catacomb Bust of Christ

Art by unknown artist (c. 4th century)

- What do you see?

- Who do you think this person is? What makes you think that?

- This artwork is a <u>mural</u>. A mural is a drawing or painting on a wall or ceiling. One of Jesus' followers created this mural on the wall of a catacomb, which is an underground tunnel.

- Tell me what you believe Jesus might be thinking or saying in this mural.

Easter

Jesus' Friends Share the Good News with the World

The first thing Jesus' friends did after being filled with the Holy Spirit at Pentecost was go out and tell the people in Jerusalem about Jesus. They wanted everyone to know the Good News about God's love.

Jesus wanted His friends to tell the whole world about what He taught them. Before He ascended into heaven, He told them:

> *"Go, therefore, and make disciples of all nations, baptizing them in the name of the Father, and of the Son, and of the Holy Spirit, teaching them to observe all that I have commanded you. And behold, I am with you always, until the end of the age."* (Matthew 28:18-20)

And that is just what His disciples did! They went out to all parts of the world and told those they met about Jesus. Some of Jesus' friends wrote down what Jesus said and did and how we can be His followers. Eventually, these writings were put together in one book called the Bible. Ever since then, Christians have shared the Good News of God's love. When we teach you about Jesus, that is what we're doing—sharing the Good News of God's love so that you can be Jesus' friend too!

What did you hear?

How do you get to know Jesus?

Does Jesus want us to share the Good News of God's love with others?

Sunrises and Sunsets

Remember that the Earth spinning, or rotating, is what causes day and night. The sun appears to be moving across the sky, but really the Earth turns and makes it look like the sun is moving.

Stand up and face away from me. Now, imagine I am the sun and you are the Earth. You are facing away from the sun, so it is night. Slowly spin around and keep your head in line with your body. When you start to see me out of the corner of your eye, stop.

When our part of Earth starts to turn toward the sun, that is the sunrise. At first, the sun barely peeks over the horizon, which is the place where the earth and sky meet. Because the Earth always turns in the same direction, the sun always rises in the east.

Now, slowly keep turning. Over the course of the day, the sun will look like it is moving across the sky, but notice that I am not moving, you (the Earth) are! When you can see me out of the corner of your eye only, stop.

As our part of Earth starts to turn away from the sun, the sun goes back down under the horizon. That is called the sunset. When you keep turning so you can't see me anymore, it's like when the sun goes below the horizon. The sun sets on our part of Earth, and it gets dark and colder. This is because there is less light and heat from the sun. Because Earth always turns in the same direction, the sun always sets in the west.

What is one thing you learned about sunrises and sunsets today?

Easter

Then Jesus approached and said to them, "All power in heaven and on earth has been given to me. Go, therefore, and make disciples of all nations, baptizing them in the name of the Father, and of the Son, and of the Holy Spirit, teaching them to observe all that I have commanded you."

-Matthew 28:18-20